T0150832

By the same author

POETRY

The Revisionist

The Astropastorals

CRITICISM

Amerifil.txt: A Commonplace Book

Lines from London Terrace: Essays and Addresses

BIOGRAPHY

Both: A Portrait in Two Parts

THE REVISIONIST

AND

THE ASTROPASTORALS

COLLECTED POEMS

THE REVISIONIST

AND

THE ASTROPASTORALS

COLLECTED POEMS

DOUGLAS CRASE

WITH AN INTRODUCTION BY MARK FORD

NIGHTBOAT BOOKS

NEW YORK

Introduction by Mark Ford

xi

THE REVISIONIST

Part One

The Revisionist

3

Part Two

America Began in Houses

17

The Day Line

19

Locale

21

The House at Sagg

22

The Lake Effect

23

Experience and What To Make of It

25

The Continent as the Letter M

29

The Elegy for New York

31

To a Watertower

33

Life in a Small Neighborhood

35

Toronto Means the Meeting Place

36

Abraham Lincoln in Cleveland

38

Heron Weather

40

Part Three

Six Places in New York State

1. SAGGAPONNACK

43

2. CUYLERVILLE

45

3. PULTNEYVILLE

47

4. THE PINNACLE RANGE

49

5. GENESEE FALLS

51

6. CHIMNEY BLUFF

53

Part Four

Creation du Monde

57

Summer

59

Great Fennville Swamp

61

In Memory of My Country

63

Whiteout

64

The Winter House

65

Replevin

67

Covenant

68

Trover

6 9

The One Who Crossed the Hudson

7 0

In Defense of Ellis Hollow Creek

7 2

Part Five

Gunpowder Morning in a Gray Room

7 7

In the Fall When It's Time To Leave

7 9

Blue Poles

8 1

Sagg Beach

8 3

Felix Culpa Returns from France

8 5

Chelsea Square

9 1

When Spring Comes First to West 21st Street

9 3

Color Peak Weekend

95

There Is No Real Peace in the World

97

THE ASTROPASTORALS

Once the Sole Province

101

A reductionism that makes the world

103

Dog Star Sale

104

Sale II

106

Theme Park

107

True Solar Holiday

108

Under the rim of maybe

110

To the Light Fantastic

111

Connecticut

113

The pays d'en haut Sublime

114

Astropastoral

115

Time: when not to come undone

117

Refuge

118

Notes

121

Acknowledgments

123

INTRODUCTION

In his resolutely unimpressed review of Hart Crane's *The Bridge* of 1930, the critic Yvor Winters insisted that what Crane's poem chiefly proved was "the impossibility of getting anywhere with the Whitmanian inspiration." "No writer of comparable ability has struggled with it before," continued Winters, "and, with Crane's wreckage in view, it seems highly unlikely that any writer of comparable genius will struggle with it again." Notwithstanding this harsh verdict, the centrality of *The Bridge* to the canon of American literature is rarely disputed these days; and Crane's epic has served as inspiration, rather than health warning, to generations of poets who have set out to wrestle, like Jacob with the angel, with the legacy of Whitman's *Leaves of Grass*.

In *The Revisionist*, published in 1981, Douglas Crase established himself as among the most resourceful, inventive, ambitious and well-equipped of those attempting to renew and extend the Whitmanian covenant. Like Crane's, his quest was for a historically layered epic that would acknowledge the multifarious, often grotesque, betrayals of the ideal of America as hymned by Whitman, and yet not succumb to skepticism or disenchantment.

I was a devoted John Ashbery aficionado—indeed had signed up to write a doctoral thesis on him under the supervision of John Bayley at Oxford University—when I acquired *The Revisionist*, a couple of years after it came out, in the course of one of my periodic "research trips" to New York, finding it on the overflowing shelves of the intoxicatingly musty Gotham Book Mart ("Wise Men Fish Here") on Forty-sixth Street. At a time when postmodernist forms of irony seemed able to undermine any attempt at authentic utterance, it was a glorious experience to ride the surge of the opening lines of Crase's title poem, and then to realize that the emotional uplift afforded by the poem's rhythmic energies was the result of no trick or gimmick, but of what Emerson called a "metre-making argument."

Emerson famously rubbed his eyes a little, "to see if this sunbeam were no illusion," while first perusing the 1855 edition of *Leaves of Grass*, dispatched to him with the compliments of the author; and *The Revisionist* excited similar exclamations of wonder from poets and critics across the spectrum when it first appeared. Here are a few extracts from the "chorus of smiles" that greeted it: "Crase has every prospect of becoming one of the strong poets of his own generation" (Harold Bloom); "*The Revisionist* seems to me an extraordinarily fine book of poems, only the more extraordinary for being a first book . . . Mr. Crase is already brilliantly the master of several distinct and identifiable idioms, all of which he uses to dramatic or comic or even shocking effect" (Anthony Hecht); "This is the most powerful first book I have seen in a long time. The thematic title poem is magnificent, proclaiming the originality which only revision can provide, finding at a late time in parts of a twilit city the highest tales of our whole country" (John Hollander); "The most interesting book of first poems in many years" (Richard Howard); "A marvelous new poet—deeply and absorbingly 'American,' unfazed by the complex sentence of our past, and already parsing a future he will help us to live" (James Merrill); "For sheer ambition, ingenuity and wit, Crase stands alone" (Jay Parini); "That Crase's invocation of the Whitmanian poetic tradition can be so powerful after all these years of overuse and abuse is a small miracle of revisionism itself" (Phoebe Pettingell); "This is a staggeringly am-

bitious book, and its author sets about his task manfully, with no bash-
fulness or false modesty" (Richard Tillinghast). It was no doubt a com-
ment by Ashbery himself, used as jacket copy, that pushed me to spring
for *The Revisionist* all those decades ago: "Crase looks at the city and
the landscape with the amused, disabused eye of a lover. Revisionism,
in his supple argumentative poetry, turns out to be something very
close to love."

Crase's title poem begins with an "If"—and it must be acknowl-
edged it's an awfully big one:

> If I could raise rivers, I'd raise them
> Across the mantle of your past: old headwaters
> Stolen, oxbows high and dry while new ones form,
> A sediment of history rearranged.

Nevertheless, despite the hypothetical manner in which it is framed,
the task the poem here sets itself is—imaginatively at least—a Her-
culean one, for its goal is a recasting of the idea of America that will
change both understanding of the country's historical record and the
prevailing sense of possibilities available to the contemporary "Amer-
ican Scholar," to borrow another concept from Emerson. The supple-
ness, to use Ashbery's term, of the argument depends not so much on
developing a logical sequence of cause and effect, as in dramatizing,
in an original and highly charged idiom, the ongoing processes of en-
gagement and participation, the ebb and flow of belonging inherent
in the idea of democracy—or at least in Whitman's figurations of de-
mocracy.

At the same time Crase is ever-conscious that it takes all sorts to
make up a *demos*, and that poetry can no more escape the uses of lan-

guage that surround it, the uses, indeed, that it models and mimics and shadows, and on which it depends, than an American citizen can escape the implications of *E pluribus unum*. In a fascinating comment on his prosody in 1987 Crase outlined his concept of "civil meter," which he defined as "the meter we hear in the propositions offered by businessmen, politicians, engineers, and all our other alleged or real professionals":

> If you write in this civil meter, it's true you have to give up the Newtonian certainties of the iamb. But you gain a stronger metaphor for conviction by deploying the recognizable, if variable patterns of the language of American power. And to say that this civil meter is a metaphor for conviction is to acknowledge that it, just like iambic measures, is a unit of artifice and one dimension of a form.

The authority admiringly noted by so many early reviewers of *The Revisionist* has, therefore, to be insistently monitored and assessed, along with the forms of complicity that it entails with the "language of American power." Much of the excitement of Crase's poetry can be traced to the self-conscious interplay that it generates between the heady impetus of its rhythmic drive—that is its meter—and the civil awareness of "artifice" that it simultaneously inculcates. Not for nothing did Crase study as an undergraduate in the School of Public and International Affairs at Princeton (1962–1966); and clearly his day job as a speechwriter for clients ranging from Eastman Kodak to General Electric has fostered in him a preternatural sensitivity to the implications and cadences of public discourse.

Only rarely, however, in a poem such as "Experience and What To Make of It," with its italicized academic markers (*Abstract ... State-*

ment of the problem ... Materials and methods ... Results ... Discussion ... etc.) does Crase approach the realms of satire. His primary mode in *The Revisionist* is a sinuous, semi-abstract landscape poetry that combines topographic and historic and political perspectives that react with each other like chemicals in an ongoing experiment; in its volatile instability, Crase's composite medium, held together only, it often seems, by his masterful syntax, is mimetic of his impatience with clichés, his restless search for new ways of conjugating our attempts to inhabit the past and the present, or to envisage the future. At moments the Whitmanian promise ("I stop somewhere waiting for you") is converted into the language of office-speak—"In every jurisdiction / And every area I promise I've already arrived." Elsewhere, following the Crane of "Repose of Rivers" or the Ashbery of "The One Thing That Can Save America," Crase is drawn to dreamy, bird's-eye views of land and nation, as in the whimsical "The Continent as the Letter M," with its nod and a wink to Wallace Stevens's "The Comedian as the Letter C":

> To the soft soil of that consonant we return
> Made Massey-Ferguson fertile and turning over
> A train of little *m*'s behind the plow. America ...

America may be the grandest of ideas, as well as a physical country, but can't it also be eyed on the most granular level, in relation to the shape of its second letter, a letter that also happens to be the first in the name of a major manufacturer of agricultural equipment, whose plows, in another rhyme, make *m*-shaped furrows in the land? Yet M is also, the poem then points out, prominent in place names derived from Native American peoples who fell victim to its European invaders—*Maumee, Menominee, Michilimackinac.* As in the "Powhatan's Daughter" section of *The Bridge,* poetic stirring of the sediment of history may expand awareness and knowledge, but it can also induce guilt and vertigo—"Deep, past Appalachian deep," Crase's poem concludes, "The inarticulate lives in its hold on me."

The Revisionist's exploration of the concept of revision is sophisticated, wide-ranging and astute. It enables Crase to position his idiom in relation to his Transcendentalist forebears, indeed to create his own late-twentieth-century version of Emersonian rhetoric, in which urgings and images whirl dizzyingly forward, while the logic supposedly undergirding their propulsive movement keeps raising then ducking its head. "Power," as "Self-Reliance" proclaims, "ceases in the instant of repose; it resides in the moment of transition from a past to a new state, in the shooting of the gulf, in the darting to an aim." Crase's syntax is the primary bearer of this display of self-reliant power, "shooting," as it does, "the gulf" between competing idioms and ideas, and insisting—or at least delicately insinuating—that both the writer and the reader (at least once she or he has "tuned in"), can be energized and boosted by the multiple transitions that the poem traces. Consider the time and space covered by this sentence, and the vision of contingency and of historical process that it parses:

It's inescapable
How history has targeted the tiniest, safest life
With the knowledge that chance and power, unmitigated,
Are always impending out of the godless distance toward it
The way there is always a comet impending toward the earth
And it's only a question now of how close and when,

A recombinant message which has breached the world
And altered the code so thoroughly that issues graceful once
As travel or turning the calendar beget features of flight,
Contortion and alarm instead.

("THERE IS NO REAL PEACE IN THE WORLD")

The phrase "godless distance" is itself a measure of the temporal and cultural gulf between Crase and such as Emerson and Whitman and Thoreau, and hence of the need for a revisionist capable of extrapolating from their belief systems what can still be of use when transplanted to the disembodying networks and information streams of secular late-capitalism.

The Revisionist, which came out when Crase was thirty-seven, ran to eighty-three pages in the original edition. Those not familiar with the contours of his career may be surprised to see that it occupies around five-sixths of this collected poems. What, such readers are likely to wonder, has Crase been up to in the decades since? Well, in 1996 he published a commonplace book entitled *Amerifil.txt* that collaged extracts from twenty-three writers, ranging in dates from John Wise (1652–1725) to John Ashbery (1927–2017); these passages were chosen for the light they cast, directly or obliquely, on "the nature of the national character," as the jacket copy put it. Eight years later appeared *Both*, a highly original double portrait of a pair of Harrow-educated English botanists called Rupert Barneby (1911–2000) and Dwight Ripley (1908–1973)—Ripley was also a poet, an artist, and a patron of institutions such as the gallery Tibor de Nagy. And in 2017 Pressed Wafer issued *two* Crase volumes: a collection of essays and addresses called *Lines from London Terrace* (London Terrace being the vast block on West Twenty-third Street in which Crase has an apartment), and *The Astropastorals*, a chapbook containing thirteen new poems. It is this chapbook that is here incorporated as the final one-sixth of Crase's poetic oeuvre. An acknowledgments note included in the Pressed Wafer edition (which sports on its cover a glorious portrait of Crase by Trevor Winkfield) revealed that the earliest of these new poems, "Once the Sole Province," appeared in 1979, and the last, "Astropastoral," in 2000.

The idea of an "astropastoral" is a curious one, and on inspection becomes, as Lewis Carroll's Alice famously put it, "curiouser and curiouser." Crase's post-*The Revisionist* poems set about applying his "civil meter" to the cosmos itself, partly, one suspects, in search of some kind of escape from the corporate hegemony that has so ruthlessly determined the horizons of American citizens in the years since Ronald Reagan came to power (the year before *The Revisionist* was published), but also as a means of articulating a global eco-consciousness. Seen from afar, the whole earth can seem a mixture of dump and refuge, as the chapbook's last lines make clear, the civil space between them increasingly imperiled:

> and the study a species
> Must turn to is that earth
> Where the dump and the refuge are relations under the sun.

Planet, sun, firmament, stars, space, heaven, the "sky's brightest body," predominate in the semantic field of the title poem, "Astropastoral," although I am not sure, despite its evocation of these interstellar perspectives, if it isn't also a coded love poem addressed to a charismatic but elusive hero-figure somewhat in the mold of The Leader in W. H. Auden's *The Orators*:

Saw you vote with your feet and hit the ground running,
Kiss the ground, rescued, and (*this wasn't a drill*)
Saw you fall to your knees on the ground
By the body of your friend on the ground
And though these fall beside you like gantries, it is
You who are rising above them and you are not there.
Like a rocket in winter, I have been there to see you
Logged in as a guest among stars . . .

Counterbalancing the galactic vistas opened up by the poems collected in *The Astropastorals* are less elevating references to pollution ("Dog Star Sale"), ammo dumps ("Theme Park"), pipelines, landfill and wasteland ("Refuge"). Those familiar with *The Revisionist* but reading these later poems here for the first time will note on occasion a certain loosening in the tightly-woven mesh of Crase's poetic idiom —four commas and a colon make up all the punctuation deployed in "Dog Star Sale," for instance, while three of the book's shortest poems come to us with no title, as if they were odd fragments of poetic material snipped and stored for future use. It is to be hoped that the poems in *The Astropastorals* will be seen as more than just a coda to the achievement of *The Revisionist*. They reveal Crase swivelling his wide-angled telescope from the earth to the heavens, and reporting back eloquently on the infinite spaces that so terrified Pascal. "Up slip creek in the dark" is how, in a quirky moment of humor, one of these poems sums up Crase's confrontation with the sublime—a region, unlike America, which no amount of revision can ever make habitable.

—MARK FORD *London, August 2019*

THE REVISIONIST

PART ONE

THE REVISIONIST

1

If I could raise rivers, I'd raise them
Across the mantle of your past: old headwaters
Stolen, oxbows high and dry while new ones form,
A sediment of history rearranged. If I could unlock
The lakes, I'd spill their volume over the till
I know you cultivate: full accumulations swept away,
The habit of prairies turned to mud. If I had glaciers,
I'd carve at the stony cliffs of your belief:
Logical mountains lowered notch by notch, erratics
Dropped for you to stumble on. Earthquakes, and I'd
Seize your experience at its weakest edge: leveled
Along a fault of memories. Sunspots, I'd cloud
Your common sense; tides, and I'd drown its outlines
With a weight of water they could never bear.
If I had hurricanes, I'd worry your beaches
Into ambiguity: barrier islands to collect them
In one spot and in another the sudden gut
That sucks them loose to revolve in dispersion with
The waves. If I had frost, I'd shatter the backbone
Of your thought: an avalanche of gravel, a storm
Of dust. And if I could free volcanoes, I'd tap
The native energies you've never seen: counties
Of liquid rock to cool in summits you'd have to

Reckon from. If I could unroll a winter of time
When these were done, I'd lay around your feet
In endless fields where you could enter and belong,
A place returning and a place to turn to whole.

2

Who wouldn't meet you in a moment that might have been
If it were only accessible and open to the public
At convenient hours? Even far off in the afternoon
I've wondered to find you waiting there tethered
And dreaming under the heart-sharp linden leaves,
A dream of an urban garden against the noise.
Beyond the newels with their stiff pineapple crowns
I have imagined my welcome in the hospitality
You extend to the lovers who use their lives up
Reconsidering you, who have seen your reflection
Light their youth and are fastened from that instant
In the track of your departing charm, whose substantial
Bodies would make you substantial and complete, firm
Of your place in history. Repeatedly, it seems
You could be there exact in a corner of privet
And ready for the perfect interview, the one in which
The arrangement of expressions and the things you say
Will embrace your sympathies line for line, and the one
Of which I tell the world, at last, you have touched time.
Not dead, not even past, in this enclosure you could

Make yourself available to me and if I haven't reached you
It doesn't mean that you are out of reach. Diligent,
As sure as I know your name, I know that you are there
Between the live honeysuckle and the cast anthemion,
Between the linden flower and the honey from the flower.

3

It is the end of April when brown thrashers arrive,
Their range being Maine, northern Michigan and southern
Manitoba south to the Gulf of Mexico: most of the uneasy
Mid-nineteenth-century United States. Their song,
Just as the Peterson *Field Guide* describes it,
Is "a succession of deliberate notes and phrases…
Usually in pairs," but their most distinctive habit
Is the one which resulted in their name, the way they forage
On the ground among dead leaves. What they like to do
Is thrash, with no trace of patience they like to thrash
Among the leaves by poking into them bill first
And whipping their heads from side to side.
If you were a worm, the sound might be deafening.
Even to me it is loud, and I have to stop to find out
Who is interrupting me. You can find them thrashing
In dry woodlands and under the shrubbery. If you live
In Brooklyn, there are thrashers in Prospect Park. But
If you don't see them, look for where they've been thrashing
In a layer of leaves, in the litter of the last few falls.

4

In every township of every county, in every location
In states and towns, my ambition wraps tighter and tighter
Around your name. In every district where there is
Restitution owing, where your riches inspired plunder
Instead of care, my outrage gathers on your interests
To give them form. Out of the asphalt in Kansas City
I will accomplish the resurrection of the Board of Trade,
Out of the parking lots of Buffalo I will recover
The Larkin Building's uncompromising piers, and
Out of the parking structures in Chicago I'll remold
The Schiller Building and the Old Stock Exchange.
Like a vengeful Johnny Appleseed I'll girdle each
Male ailanthus tree and like a Know-Nothing I'll close
The ports to chestnut blight and the Dutch elm disease.
Merciless, I will rip the museum and the zoo
From Central Park, I will excise the Transamerica
From San Francisco, I will sever the interstate
At the mouth of Chesapeake Bay. Immediate, I will break
The 1811 grid that imprisoned New York, I will reopen
McCulloch v. *Maryland* to honor the offended states,
I will expose the payoff that humbled Tilden
And reduced the Union victory via President Hayes.
Remote or present, I have seen you traded through public
And private hands until every account against you
Excites me to personal revenge. (I will expel the five-
Million-dollar Velasquez and bring the Jackson Pollock

Home.) I can see that my intervention is required,
The more urgently as your prospects alter and disappear.
I will have to be your guarantee. If you're out of place
I'll have to give you place, and if you're out of time
I'll have to lift you into mine. As you are dispersed,
Return and inhabit me. In every jurisdiction
And every area I promise I've already arrived.

5

What I am after to remember is not what was,
And what I am anxious to save is not the same
For in the moment I saw you, you were changed.
In the most intimate of fields you may
Never have been known, and in the most natural
Of flowers it's possible to read the account
Of my interferences instead. Together,
I thought we were having an honest childhood
Of daisies, dandelions and Queen Anne's lace
Only to discover these come wrapped tightly
In the same colonial history as my own. Together
I thought we were fragrant of spearmint, chicory
And the multiflora rose only to find these
Were fugitive as the others who came to give you
The recognizable smell of home. I wasn't surprised
To learn about starlings showing their muscle
In the park, or the fifty English sparrows

That flew for their freedom above the bay;
I can understand the pigeons who pack themselves in
In their own communities: the habits of birds
Are big in their motions like a man's, and it makes
Sense that in sixty years the starling, shoving
The bluebird aside in the process, could have
Reached the Bering Sea. But the plants, so subtle
As they reproduce I can't even tell when they
Accomplished it, so firmly attached to their own
Kind of earth that I envy them their "roots" in one
Of my favorite metaphors, who would expect it
Of the plants which are, after all, the very look
Of you? Knapweed, mullein, butter-and-eggs:
They came bouncing along on covered wagons, riding
The stagecoach, settling in the dust behind
The railroads. Loosestrife, the purple filler
At the low end of the field, came vagabonding
In the wool of distant English sheep and docked
At a Hudson River factory and now the Japanese
Lady's thumb, having arrived as a stowaway
With the china, packed in straw, is deftly
Fulfilling its version of manifest destiny.
The motion that finds you, the motion you were,
These have combined so I may never untangle
Their effects. The broad pastures going west
To provide my eye's first frame of you, provided
Also the avenue which ragweed and black-eyed Susan
Would follow east in a journey that made them

Synonymous with its edge. The heat of the fires
Which burned over your logged-out heart released
The seed of the jack pine and gave it a delayed
But native start. The moment I saw you my natural
Love began, twisting and turning, to love you
The more the way you were and as I complicated you.

6

Even in separation, the grace of potential union
Spills around us to indicate how my course of action,
Freed from the peculiar moment which pointed it here
Or there, could have widened in other directions
Toward the horizon: the real one, the 360-degree
Horizon I have to turn around for in order to see.
It's an ample limit, but always sure of being there:
A rim of temporal capacity that closes in behind me
Just as I think I'm escaping forward in a straight line.
People are fond of saying there's no turning back
But, for me at least, this is true only in the sense
That "back" follows me no matter where I turn. It comes
Lifting you with it so every encounter, my every move,
Winks of your not-so-distant authority, of the world
We could have created a degree or two away. In fact,
It hardly seems necessary to speak of turning back
When sideways would do so well: there you are,
In exactly the position and within the same horizon

That a defter course of action would have brought us to
By now. Though we never reached it together, this world
We planned is the only one in which I can imagine you.
As a result, and despite our separation, I have never
Relented my right to plot the coordinates which might
Have got us here, so that even my memories of you *as is*
Take shape in the width of once possible days.

7

It wasn't a real season when I saw you last.
Between clouds maybe, because the sun makes me
Remember it as if autumn was rattling
In the air: it was only California though.
It could've been fall, but I'd need a calendar
To tell. It seemed to be winter when we came
Through Donner Pass, chains on the tires
Because of all the snow. It was, as you said,
Worth it after all: the view from the top
Of one of those hills, Russian or Telegraph,
Or looking back at night from a Central Street
Picture window in Sausalito. Yes, it was
Just as you said it would be, all amethyst
And pearls, and I didn't need to be convinced
Of your thesis that life could take place
More beautifully in a beautiful place. No,
I knew all along you'd figure a way to remain

And that I'd return overland the way we came,
Through the vast states that entered the Union
At various times, past the little towns
Empty of population and holding their names
On metal sticks at the side of the road:
Fair Haven, Buena Vista, Pleasant View.

8

The canal rubs up against the railroad
As if it always had, without a trace of the engineering
That made it possible to shoulder the water to one side
And raise the thruway in its bed. Because the course
Was so narrow, the river itself has been moved
And now the four of them are crowded bunk to bunk
Through the same channel used by meltwater floods
To escape from one glacier and before the next.
The trees succeed one another too, orderly at first,
And with the leapfrog logic of fashion ever since:
The locusts were planted in Locust Valley, the elms
Lined up along their avenues to die. The canal loses
Its dimensions in a lake beneath which the salt beds
Go down a half a mile; rows of pipeline push forward
Beside the train tracks removing brine. The switches
Are idle: I have seen rusted sidings sink under
The asphalt approach to a loading dock and disappear.
On Sundays the canal locks fill with pleasure craft,

Off and on. The phlox blooms wildly about the towpath,
The little flags sputter in the sun. The scenery
From one old mountain to another—road, railroad,
River and canal in a watergap the settlers called
"The Noses"—mounts up in a natural frame to be
Observed: everything allows itself to be seen again
In the focus of its possibilities. Although the past
Seems to be level in its place there's room for more
And the ragged additions polish the previous days.

PART TWO

AMERICA BEGAN

IN HOUSES

Unlike the other countries, this one
Begins in houses, specific houses and the upstairs room
Where constitutions vibrate in the blockfront drawers,
A Queen Anne highboy, or maybe the widow's walk
On a farmhouse hundreds of miles inland and believed
By the family to be a lookout for Indians though clearly
It was a pioneer's conceit, fresh as the latest politics
From home: so much for that innocent thesis *The Frontier*.
No, between the houses and the people living in them
Ought to be a view as easy to pick out from the road
As the traditional six-over-six of a double window sash,
And just as functional. Occasionally, when this meeting
Of artifice and artifact occurs, a national monument
Is declared, but to visit it afterward is invariably
To be dismayed: could they really have planted lilacs
By the door, had Sheraton sideboards when they were the rage,
Stenciled the dining room till only the wainscot
Had been spared? How touchingly people embrace the styles
Which look in retrospect like individual good taste.
Still, they lived with them and that was long enough
That it continues having its effect. It's been said
Of a house that it's the carapace of a soul: perhaps,
But not always of the occupant any more than the shell

Of a hermit crab can be said to be his own. It takes
Some growing into, or making over, here and in the houses
Scattered one by one in individual commonplace yards.
The squirrels come in on the wires, bringing their news.
The lilacs move over first for spruce and lately, everywhere
One looks, for rhododendrons. Strangely, as the pilgrim
Aspirations increase they seem to diminish in promise
Yet who can say that out of these borrowed fashions
Won't come a suburban mutant enlarging nature
Once again. The Federal fanlight opens in the sun
And on the gateleg table is a treaty to be signed.

THE DAY LINE

Beyond any vision of a Northwest Passage
Or of its usefulness, the river endures to tease us
Reach by reach with prospects of an extended world
And not its narrow origins. Surely it leads us
As a log dropped into this subterfuge of tide
Will be seen to ride inland off the bow. The salt line
Gulls us on and windless hours are diverted
Doting on the sea-like stir: the tide on one shore
Makes earlier, hangs later on the other than it should,
And this in reports to patrons is said to prove
A confluence of oceans may be near. Each gap
In the highlands ahead brings down the sky
In promises through which the enterprise will any day
Twist into the unrestrained sweetness
Of a less empirical world. Impossible treasures
Gather in tributary streams to swell the edifice we
Richly prophesy. Listen to the progress of our dreams,
The wild rain beating on the deck, the plunging steel
With which we severed the unbelieving hands.
In this passage we are stately as though invincible
And the breeze has come before us with offerings.
The crew long since given over to the air,
More beguiling by the hour, now dreams transfixed
Of the valley responsible for grafting these perfumes

On such distances. At every pass it is more difficult
To remember the mission as it was charged. Here,
And one must move slowly as we are to understand,
Here on green banks is nothing new but this,
Undefended except for savages, what's left of Eden.

LOCALE

The sound of it is always there,
The fumbling of pigeons in the old barn:
You'd think first of the wind
But it's too specific of origin for that,
At the same section of unused pulley track
High in the peak where an open window was.
It is like that, interrupted now and then
By the flap of exits and entrances,
Settling down sometimes in the burr
Of a plump snooze, but never stilled,
Though when I try to make it out
It's dim as the pigeons in the mow and gray.
It follows me and I suppose I've encouraged
The attention—when it goes faint
I try to listen harder, when it is loud
I stare up at the bright dust to see
Where it is coming from. For something
Which is part of life it's attached
In a funny way and yet there's no danger
Of it ever flying off to someplace else.
If it wasn't for the racket the elevator
Makes, the thump of wet bales falling
In the haymow, you'd hear what I mean.
At night when the barn is vacant as the moon
It will be unmistakable in the loft,
Its ruffling outskirts tentative,
A tentative nest at an immanent remove.

THE HOUSE AT SAGG

The way the physical things add up,
The plain practical shapes of them derive
A mounting architecture in which the minutes
Reach for footing, solid enough
To hold them down. Our bodies, of course, but also
The space they agitate in a just right bed,
The doorways that make you stoop and the ones that don't,
The advantages of a sunken living room:
These things push the living in or out of shape
And, like the climber rose on the trellis,
It longs to contend with them. The simple things
(The heat of the water in the tap) exist,
And in their measurements is a way for the living
To emulate their still extent. Properly put together,
The things we touch are announced in the ones we do:
The driveway, built of pebbles, rattles accordance
With how and how often it's disturbed. Beautiful,
Our actions depend on finding their objects
And growing around them
Until one or the other is forced to bloom.

THE LAKE EFFECT

So many versions at any time are all exemplary
(In fog, suspended drops of rain; in a blizzard,
Each driven crystal the authentic apotheosis of the snow)
It is impossible to choose, to even want to choose
From millions of improbably accurate identities,
Things as they are. Selection magnifies, but concurrently
It excludes and how can that be satisfactory
When present estates, so-called, include all recollections
Of what they were as well as the motives for remembering them?
This being true, which past is agreeably the one
For bringing the looks of the world up to date?
Even though there's nothing new to say about it,
The weather isn't suspected of offering a clue
And this despite the attention paid to minutest variations
On the compact barometric scale. Slowly, popular wisdom
Seems to have lost its weather-canny sense
(When the geese are arguing it means unseasonable storms)
In favor of a new vocabulary in which a stationary low
Sets up its unmistakable loitering fronts of gloom.
Big words like "spring" are hardly useful for telling
What's about. When the wind comes over the warmer lake
The troubled surfaces don't stand a chance: an incident
Of water can be gigantically transformed and brought to land
In altitudes that seem to belie its origin. In trillions
And trillions the universe of surpluses descends

So that in comparison even the very air is remembered
As once being seen in form, though what that was
Now no one is able to say. No wonder in such a country
The soul goes mad, keen to the rappings underfoot
In wooden towns, the tablets of gold that are known to glow
On the dreary hills outside. Energies of terrible belief
Have to appear: temperance, drunkenness hold camp meetings
Close at hand. These are ways to combat velleity
But still the level weather shifts and comes
And, without leaving the earth, no one sees clearly
Through its cover to the sun. It's not that visibility
Is poor but that so much so visible must be perceived
Vastly obscure. The underinflated days weigh indistinct
As the lidded atmosphere, and only the untenable instant
Is separate from the muffled expanse it anxiously regards
And into which it once again subsides.

EXPERIENCE AND WHAT

TO MAKE OF IT

Accepted for publication and reprinted. *Abstract*:
Isolates of significance from randomly selected fields
Of experience proved tolerant to previously effective
Means for their control. Segregation of progenies
Demonstrated tolerance is emotionally determined.
Segregation ratios indicate more than one emotion
Is involved. Infinite mutations of high tolerance
Appear now to be possible. *Statement of the problem*:
Since its inception in such and such a year, capacity
For experience has been bewildered by the landmarks of
Spent meanings, finding the way among them no easy task
As, like trees blazed by advancing pioneers, they show
Not only the way, they show this way and that. Further,
Each time in the act of turning over a new leaf
The scab of significance has also been exposed, stuck
Like a parasite already there. Against this infestation
Of meaning it was necessary to establish a program
Of control: Say that all experience is of equal value
Or all experience equally meaningless, follow the line
Of least resistance, and the unblemished best may be picked
From among their row—a harvest clean of smut or mildew,
Incidents shiny and firm as in a basket of wax fruit.
This selectivity in experience isn't a bad control,

Call it the "ostrich" method if you want to, sticking
Your head in the sand, but it saves a lot of grief.
Lately, however, something is going wrong and failure
To control significance on experience by avoiding it
Has been noted by more than one observer (you, me,
Friends et al., this year). The occurrences reported
In this paper all took place. The objective was
To verify that the staying power of significance
Is due to emotional resilience and is with present
Knowledge beyond control. *Materials and methods*:
Cuttings of experience (slices of life) were taken
From virgin fields and analyzed to ensure no personal
Significance had yet attached. These were allowed
To incubate at memory settings up to several years.
Repetition of each experience was made under conditions
Closely approximating life and the effects, or progeny,
Compared to the previous time around. Determinations
Were replicated as often as the subject could endure.
Results: Significance was discovered in all cases
To have attached itself with pathogenic consequences
By the time of second experience. Thus a rearrangement
Of the room took on significance because of the initial
Arrangement of the room, even when the first was but
Haphazard. Significance was found to sporulate profusely
Under conditions of comparison and contrast as, for example,
A growing mustache engendered political connotations
From its previous absence. Once attached to the second-
Generation experience, significance proved resistant

To all efforts to dislodge it. A record played once
Was crisp as a new dollar bill but on repeated attention
Sagged with first association despite all attempts
To avoid a recurrence of the conditions under which
It was first heard. Moreover, recordings from the same
Composer's works, never yet heard, were found to be
Similarly affected the moment they reached the subject's
Ears. *Discussion*: The emotions, securely programmed
To reproduce according to some sort of genetic code
Of their own, seem likely to survive an avoidance
Of host experience for however prolonged a period
One can choose, reestablishing their unwanted meanings
On cue at the first reappearance of the familiar act.
Or in the interim there may occur among them the deft
Reshuffling of a feeling here or there, like chromosomes,
To produce a vigorous mutant otherwise unchanged
Except in its vital capacity for hitching a ride
On just the experiences transferred to in order
To shake the preceding significance of others off.
Though not conclusive, the findings reported suggest
There are infinite mutations of this latter sort
Still to appear. Investigators should expect each new
Experience, no matter how bright, to brown at the edges
And curl under the certain attack of meaning if only
Because of the contrast its own appearance brings about.
Thus, though all experience is equally meaningless,
The price of having it is meaning, and adoption
Of the ostrich or "know-nothing" position would appear

To work only temporarily in controlling its inevitable
Import. Clearly, better controls are called for
But until they are forthcoming the best to be done
Is go on with the harvest expecting intermittent relief
From infection and nothing more. *Tables of evidence*.

THE CONTINENT

AS THE LETTER M

Think of it starting out this way: in profile
Two almost immediate peaks, but widely opposite,
The basin humming with weather in between
And approaching speech as summary ineffectual
As the oceans beside its feet, their murmuring
Montauk, at Monterey. Think of the central
Organizing mound of it, around which
An alphabet of fir mounts up to fall away
Just at the timberline, the solid crown of it
When seen from cabin windows, imposing crash sites
Seen from stricken planes. Ponderous,
The name of our country is ponderous and brown,
Laborious as a growing mastodon, its own huge shoulders
The only thing it's hanging on. Columbia,
Paumanok, say it, the Alamo—we build
Outward from this middle interior sound
So far until, unsupported,
Our imaginations begin to let us down.
To the soft soil of that consonant we return,
Made Massey-Ferguson fertile and turning over
A train of little *m*'s behind the plow. America:
So many centuries thicken its animal sound,

This mammoth that holds us between its knees,
Maumee, Menominee, Michilimackinac,
Deep, past Appalachian deep
The inarticulate lives in its hold on me.

THE ELEGY FOR NEW YORK

The buildings are at their stations, untimely
On the tick of property which can always assemble
To a bid. The air rights fidget about the vents,
Zoning and setback line up to be invested in. Today
The last holdout on the block was satisfied in brick,
Six derelict kittens moved blind to their rescue
Along nth Avenue, and the once individual rooms
Close rank in a take-it-or-leave-it portfolio:
Solid front. Steam rises from beneath the street
No higher than the metal cornices, applications
Were filed this afternoon, my days in the city
Made ready to appear (stretcher to header as dear
As Flemish bond and tiny among the derricks and drawn
Cranes). I arrived in the visible city to look for you
Where "time becomes visible with shape," as someone said.
With *shape*?
                  Each hour on the place will throw
Its sediment, the quarries are spent, the fortunes
Piece by bay in the scrapyard, numbered,
No questions asked. I've known travertine faces
Torn from a rich entablature and rushed out of town
To landfill the planned communities nearby.
Their kitchens gleam on a soil of terra-cotta winks
And smiles. In the Home and Garden Center
They have pressed-wood paneling on hand: old mill,

Old barn, and gothic oak. The Animal Hospital
Lengthens and opens its doors. From time to time
On their errands they see you (dripping with gravity
As if you were another world) hesitate over
The parkway's edge, recoil, and burst outrageous
As before to riddle Connecticut, light-years off,
With the unkempt traffic of a star.

TO A WATERTOWER

Yes, the facilities are breaking down
And why shouldn't you be concerned? Because
You live in them as in any calendar
Whose months have spalled, whose holidays
Have tipped screw-if like crippled finials.
Propped up, things never are the same,
The same for dates as gargoyles or for laws
With the deference sold out from under them.
My century, you totter on economy,
Formed on its function in a way to prove
Form truly follows function—to the dump
Or dim terrace of some urban homesteader.
                              Guest of that household,
Be seated here on cornice or on architrave
And remember how these were the neighborhoods
That won the war. Whoever expected
They would be beautiful? "It took us a week
To get the mortar off." "She laced
The quiche." Hello, little brave civilities
(Cavetto, both cymas) who blink
From beneath the vinca and paper plates;
How to address you who ought to be bordering
Avenues, stories high, instead of flowerbeds?
Yet the good of it is when any old chunk
Is saved, I suppose, and can therefore believe

In the saving grace of plunder, even,
Even when plunder redeems piecemeal.
Don't I feel safe with this graceful lawyer
And his wife, *our kind*, on their exemplary,
Pious patio? My century, in living memory
I know there were flags that thundered
To your far continuum and soldiers,
One from every class, who dressed right
To the bar of your resolve, but, ANNI
MIRABILES, these were the marble years
None can afford, uninterrupted, on their own.
You, you are under an acid rain,
A skyline more notable for the gaps in it,
A history, the too many places
Where much of the sky shows through.

LIFE IN A SMALL

NEIGHBORHOOD

It has to be an act, almost a European thing
Tricked out of its boundaries to appreciate
What is sufficient if not just enough.
And it probably must be the cat of behavior
Trained, that will slip and step through
Yet still accumulate rather than leave behind,
Accumulate content out of the cracks
Got through, imperial, empire on the sly.
It will need to accumulate to persuade,
By persuasion making a place for itself,
Survived. Its rules are brief and it knows
When it is tired, how far the border is
And the distance it can cover in twenty-four hours.
Knows, too, where neutral country may be found.
In action it is the review of what it knows,
A review of process and due possibility,
Preceding its palace of results. A palace
Where life had been possible, as it turns out.

TORONTO MEANS

THE MEETING PLACE

This is an age where limits are required.
Douane: The first twenty dollars are duty free,
After that it depends how long you stay
And certain things are better undeclared.
In a meeting place people understand the terms
Though it's acceptable if they want to pretend
They don't, as in: "Why are you holding me?"
Do you want to put a Canadian out of work?

When the Huron brought furs the Iroquois
Gave them flint. Economies briefly stabilized
But eventually they had to come to terms:
They slaughtered the Huron
And drove the Ojibway farther north.

The frontier moves. We were nostalgic
Because it disappeared but the frontier moves.
It cuts inland, it darts behind a lake, it lies
In wait for us in places where we've been.
We will turn someday and we will deal with it.
There are frontiers everywhere. I never
Expected, for instance, to find you here.
It's a nickel on your dollar, sir. Important,
Important to agree on the medium of exchange.

In a meeting place people decide on the exchange:
The Iroquois needed the furs to give to the Dutch
To get the guns to slaughter the Huron with,
Though this is disputed by modern historians.

Look, there are limits to what I require
You to believe. A meeting place means
You'll be able to pretend if the exchange
Takes place in the limits you're meeting within.
But where shall they be? The blue hollow
That turns in your turning wrist,
The edge of a lie I offered you,
The smell of your body behind a flannel shirt?
A meeting place is distinguished
By these things, a sense of the limits limiting
The exchange. These limits apprise you
Of where things are likely to end. Desired,
You must find where these limits begin.

ABRAHAM LINCOLN

IN CLEVELAND

Dead center: it's one of a thousand capitals
In this abstract territory of ours, its dominant
Structure departing, arriving, as if a terminal
Was the best that anyone could do. There are people
Living here, borderless though at the very edge
Of things, and we understand the public monument was
Meant to suggest "history" instead of commemorating
Openly that the event doesn't seem to have ever
Happened here. Yet things must have happened somehow
Even so: the department store was once an opera house,
Fat trains moved for a hundred years, the river's been
Altered by Republic Steel. Perhaps things only happen
When they stop: the crowd is there sobbing to admit
The somber train, will close around the engine where
It shivers releasing steam. In the photographs
The procession has come to a halt, the draperies
Open to discharge the lush import we were waiting for
And in this ceremony we can indulge ourselves until
The unfailing funeral begins again to overtake
Our lovely country where the streets are emptier
For being so well lit. At night after work we see how
The white people are beginning to disappear, starting out
In their cars to count the impersonal miles they were

Never content to make their own. It's true, the terrible
Body stopped here on its way to a living grave,
Gathered mourning around it as it went and left
For us this bared unbearable heart with the logic
Gone out of it: one of thousands to be built
All alike across the indecipherable land from which
Every road leads home and none is getting there.

HERON WEATHER

The terrace is empty, which shows how flat it is
When the things living next to it have been pruned:
The privet will let the day through, or the fog,
The water will soon be off, the willows amputated
Just below the solstice in the air. At evening,
The geese are so close it sounds like the moon
Has come to a cool blue boil and slipped its orbit,
Passing in migratory complaint. The cover crop
Went in too late: already the field gleams as if
It felt the undertow. Down by the pond, the developers
Have a permit from themselves to build:
No millrace, no barns, no reason for being there
Except the view—which is simultaneously flushed
From its nest for good like a frightened rail.
The builders will leave before the people moving in,
Who have no way to remember what they displace.
Three hundred and fifty years, and it still takes
Only one election to renovate the country by surprise.
The cloud front is piling up with birds, tugging at
Things I never thought would be among the ones to go.
The heron was on his island to be approached until
At the last moment the past broke ahead of the present,
Unattained, and things breathe of after, *after*,
Before even unfolding their wings.

PART THREE

SIX PLACES IN
NEW YORK STATE

1. SAGGAPONNACK

FOR ROBERT DASH

Yesterday sixty Episcopal ladies passed through the place
On tour. You have to wonder, was it important
They noticed the shipwrecked timbers which beam up
The studio from when it used to be a barn, or only
Important that their guidebooks said they would? I'm not
Sure about this, but it might be worth it to point out
That timber grows slowest when you're thinking of it,
So shipwrecks strike me personally as a good thing and
The material that comes sliding out of them is preferable
To almost anything indigenous to now. It's partly,
Of course, that the climate is to blame: the ocean
Not only surrounds us on both sides, it meets in the middle, too,
Because half the ocean is the ocean air. The water tests and
Pushes, but the air can reach over the island with a shrug.
It's devastating to think about the results. You still say
You're coming to get away, you like the sound of it so much.
It's a good example of the lengths you'll go to when you're
Really stubborn for external surroundings for a week.
Wouldn't you think you'd see the progressive reduction

To rough grasses, concealed ticks, and sand? But the light
Comes in between the timbers of the ship, which is why
You think your Airedale looks like that. One of the first
Things they did was wait a hundred years for those timbers
To arrive. Overhead, things look secure enough, but imagine
Hauling up Sagg Road with the salt water squelching in your boots
And hoisting that precious salvage into the shape of your studio.
I wonder if it was first come first serve at the wreck, or if
The elders divided their providence with the same stern arrogance
You use to divide the external from the other blue.
It's important, I guess, that the guidebook said you would,
That the Episcopal ladies came, too, to get away, that we
Never had a massacre and the only witch on record was sent
Away to Salem for her trial. After a few hundred years
A shipwreck becomes a way of seeing things. Inland, they say,
Are Iroquois and, more than likely, that's where they lie.

2. CUYLERVILLE

It will be essential to ruin their crops in the
ground and prevent their planting more.
—George Washington to General John Sullivan, 1779

There's more than one way to look at a place and this
Is one of them: you can imagine the landscape for what
It must have been (*that* feature, *this* one, these same
Horizons were really here, the circumstance of invasion
As it came). That oak was a sapling near their farthest
Town, "a hundred and twenty-eight houses mostly large
And elegant," where the lieutenant like you was getting
His firsthand look for the first time, caught skinning
The Iroquois boys for saddlebags. "The Indians, having
Punished him sufficiently, made a small opening in his
Abdomen, took out an intestine which they tied to the
Sapling, and drove him around it till he had drawn out
The whole of his intestines"—tortures, said the General
In his report, not to be mentioned out of decency,
Though it's no secret how important they are to you
In proportion as you break them loose from their first
Dull loyalties. You see, it's partly the place but
Partly the way of discovering it, so these are a good
Illustration of the double-barreled nature of your
Attachment now. The usual gauntlet of preliminaries
Has occurred but you should expect the novelty to increase
As proof of your own similar involvement comes unwound.

45

One has to marvel at how an intestine could emerge,
Iridescent when you see it in the sun, and be still joined
In rich dark to you at its other end. We don't know
The exact manner of fixing it to this tree but the effect
As you're put through your paces, the eventual unraveling,
That is, will be the same. It's a good lesson in how
Things look from an orbit as it narrows, how things feel
Being reeled in by the bewildering tug of your own insides.
Apparently there's nothing you can do; it's as though
These transplanted membranes move of their own accord
Toward the light, fasten for dear life upon the spot,
Smooth gut devoted to deciduous xylem tube. There's
No way to guess the time each individual case can easily
Involve, because of the role intestinal fortitude may play,
But the characteristic responses remain the same and as
Life in the organism erodes away the grass becomes slick
With its visceral wash—irredeemable drift—in a rank
Alluvial fan on the valley floor. It should give you
Something to think about whether you're staying or only
Stopping off to see the place, this clear interior,
So beautiful it turns you inside out to look at it.

3. PULTNEYVILLE

There's a sign at the lake which says *First White Men*
And I think it makes sense to be amused because it's
About the only sign of men, this time of year
At least. Even in season there were fewer tourists
As the water got so high, and this way along the lake
Promontories as well as the houses perhaps of friends
Were washed away for good. Angry littoral owners
Lay the blame on the joint commission where it belongs
And, of all the plausibilities, it seems the one
Most likely to make itself at home. Local interest,
Frankly, receded back across Lake Road; erosion
May be faster than it looks but it's one of the family,
Like Labor Day, and you settle in with it relieved
As soon as the newcomers have gone. This is how
The hamlet looked last year: these leaves, this sky,
The same legato lake. You can imagine bonfires
Making small-town smoke without running afoul
Of even the latest ordinance: an unlikely place
For a phantom to arise. Still, I can remember the event
As if it happened here, a "Phantom gigantic
Superb" laying down his preposterous conditions.
Probably you've thought of it yourself; it's a
Coincidence I'd like if I were you, having your feet
On the shore as a kind of birthright to begin with.

It would do nice things for my sense of symmetry
To picture the old man on Long Island, looking your way
And pleased to see this lakeside of local orchards
Has taken hold. But there aren't many who know when
They've been vindicated by their own charm, and thus
His question with the little spine in it instead:
"Whose handiwork is this?" Of course you have the right
To remain silent, but there are enough tattles around
To put you both in your places and then discuss
How you got there to boot. Eventually one of them
Will drive out to Sodus and be astonished by
The constant lake, filling in for the land which
Has failed to advance. Ontario, he will later write,
Is the blue collision which gives the shore its name,
And in the long run this speculation will be accurate
Since it's the larger one. What's missing is this
Picture of your mother from last fall, her scarves
Shivering and the leaves drawn up about her feet
In the feeblest levees on the lawn. It was her way
Of doing what she could and, never mind appearances,
You have adopted it. Of course there's more to
Your story, but this could be enough all by itself;
This shore, high water, and the slightest leafy dikes.

4. THE PINNACLE RANGE

FOR THOMAS SPENCE SMITH

When it comes to wisdom, I think it's time to consider
The arrangements our radical elders made with words.
Their effect has been enormous, though incremental,
The way the dracaena's shape is slowly but surely
Changed according to its new position at the window.
For example: "Happiness makes up in height for what
It lacks in length" has been around so long we turn
In its familiar direction unannounced, as if it could
Keep us warm or make us grow. Isn't it possible, however,
That its sense of warmth and light comes less from
Energetic meaning and more from the symmetry of consonants
Supplied? If you think about the assumptions required
By this one Yankee cleverness you're likely to find them
Questionable at best. Is happiness a high? Then what
Are these beautiful boundaries for? These lilacs are
The borders of the world and within them you can foster
The spreading repetitions of each smooth thought. These
Roses are the reaches of the place in which the most
Fantastic regional nativities can recur. The day will
Widen out to fill its space, lighting dogwood, catalpa,
Your favorite Hyde Park mug, this cat called "certain
Putten" kneading your forearm with her paws: the richest
Behavior is rich with recurrences. So you can see
What my quarrel with the quoted notion is: its crucial

Words have been transposed. Happiness, in fact, is
Defined by modesty and revealed in length; you can
Measure it by sitting still and watching the concentric
Circles form, each circle always at a different stage
Though starting here at this same origin. Tomorrow
Perhaps you'll cut the lawn or take the brightest
Tomatoes from the vine, and even as you harvest one
The next comes ripe while another forms around its
Central flower: so many tomatoes possible yet this year.
By now you can almost believe there's a "spirit of
Place"—another radical array of words—working in
Your favor here. But if it's here, what's it residing in?
The surrounding egocentric town? The dormant fever
That drove the first settlers off in waves? Or the
Insistent wisteria heading for the door. One thing's
For sure: to know the place you have to disturb it
With your touch. It's like the serenest lake, and it's only
When you finally drop the stone that the ripples suggest
The underwater esker and moraine. In the quiet impact
There are even repetitions to survey, essential
Explorations to give you the sense you have, your sense
Of so much motion coming out of this still life.

5. GENESEE FALLS

FOR RICHARD REISEM

Nothing is ever over in a place like this, which is one
Of the reasons why people come to look at it. As an
Exhibit the waterfall is naturally unsurpassed: part of
Its fascination must be in the way it demonstrates how
An event can be still permanent when it depends for its
Definition on continually going over the edge. You can
Look for some break in the action if you want, some least
Visible hint that what you're seeing isn't motion but
The separate frames suggesting it; you won't find it, though.
There are variations, to be sure—the shadows migrating
With the regularity of geese up and down the gorge—
But the important thing, the smooth identifying bend
Incurred as the water, slipping from ponderous limestone
To slight gray air, begins (or just begins) to fall,
That constant feature never disappears. No matter how
Diminished or exaggerated the river is, you can count on
Coming here to get this permanent gravitational display.
It's not even astonishing anymore, until you think of
How many ways the river might have gone. It begins,
For example, on the Allegheny Plateau and winds up where
The St. Lawrence does, but half an inch further south
And it would end in New Orleans instead, substantially
Unchanged. Or look at it like this: there shouldn't
Really be a waterfall here at all except a glacial deposit

Happened to get in the way, deflecting the river toward
This weak spot in the shale. The more time passes, the more
The possible courses that are revealed. It's your discovery
Of potential in modern times that makes a statement
Like Ralph's astonishing: "People fall into the things
They do." Up here on this bridge you know what gravity
Means, 114 feet from the bottom of the gorge, yet
Some have endured it as well as others and still survived.
With your Leica you're like a reporter on the scene,
Angling for perspective as the accident obligingly recurs.
The results go up on illuminators sometime soon, the
Show put together, the script finally cued, a permanent
Look for a never-ending event will be achieved: it's as if
A park of transparencies could be made. You already
Know what your favorite shot will be: from the east bank,
Sighted down on the bridge where a patch of light appears
Off balance, about to take the plunge. If we put it up front
It will make a nice jumping-off point for the speaker
When the lights go down. You're good at this sort of thing
So the production will be smooth, the focus excellent,
And when the lights come back up on schedule someone
Will say, "How'd it go over?", as if it was.

6. CHIMNEY BLUFF

Here, where you didn't expect it, is the highest point
On the deepest lake, a modest elevation which nonetheless
Provokes a satisfactory surprise: there's no need for
Reviewing more of the shore than this. From your current
Position you can see the wide spaces between the waves;
Far from "trooping" toward you, the waves seem to come
Distracted, slow, breaking apart in separate accidents
On the narrow beach. You can see why a place like this
Might have been sacred to the Cayugas, and there's something
Reassuring about that even though none of us knows for sure.
There was a time when you thought the meaning of such spots
Was necessary for survival, that it could be peeled off
Like the bark of a paper birch and used to transport us
In swift canoes past the hostile Iroquois. But your efforts
Convinced you at last that what's indigenous is also
By nature recalcitrant: the canoes were a lost art and
The ensuing confrontation failed to smoke out any prophecies.
So there you were after the calamity, disappointed to find,
Despite your investment of "blood, sweat, and tears," that
There was no more meaning returned than was there before.
Perhaps you thought it was useless to go on, that the most
You could do was stand there marking time, that you had
Reached, too early, the interminable final phase. I might
Be nice and say it was all part of your progress here
But of course you could have missed this place just as
You've missed so many others along the way. Yet here you are,

And what you make of the occasion will be inevitable,
Knowing you. The edges aren't secure, but they are safe:
The withered clay is hunched in great shoulders against
The wind. Given the cloud cover that prevails, the bluffs
Appear as gray, and only in the late afternoon or dawn
When the light comes in horizontally are the startling
Intricacies revealed. On the map it says the place is
"Undeveloped" but this beautiful erosion didn't happen
Overnight. Life curries its own patterns as it goes,
Dislodging first a pebble, a hunk of clay, the roots
Of a smooth dumb beech. You seldom see it happening,
Which explains why people don't wish on erosion the way
They do on shooting stars; yet it's there, tracing
Delicate downfalls when your back is turned.
It's enough to come up on it suddenly like this,
To recognize its brilliant irregularities
And be left living—the sufficient remainder.

PART FOUR

CREATION DU MONDE

Next to the argument it begins
Love's nothing, though it have its monuments
And these be heroic back there as in a park
Or at the foot of a long avenue. Take ours (that date
Like a Roman arch when stone and keystone met
To frame this vista I can't throw off, of you
In the projectable colonnade of your career)—for ours
Is proof that however the scenery honors you
Today's bright polyethylene flag also appears,
Unflappable, and isn't this the way it was to be,
Seductive per diem, to train that faith toward heaven
Which is fast on earth, upright for love? In perspective
It was easy being taken in by promises that reached
Beyond their ads, by windows dressed in the best tease
Of you, loss leader of all one always wished
To learn. No wonder when some are traded up to terms
They can barely now afford, or if I contemplate
Through impressions of almost everything that value
Which started to recede the moment your viewpoint
Fixed on me and I was trained. Be proud of me!
Deep in these aisles of commerce, among high-rise
Counters lighted on every side, I want no more
Than appreciates my fidelity—dear offshoot
Of what you meant for me. Is it my fault one finds
It everywhere, inseparable from the various things

There are: some scorned, some seized at once, most
Only to be flirted with? The planes pace upriver
Forty to the hour; the *Aglaonema*, far from China,
Blooms; and at closing time the red star crowds
Outdoors on shopping bags. How, in your memory,
Could anyone foresee the lot so plentiful
Now Stuff on the one hand and Guff on the other
Lean perpetually forward and never quite strike
The bell. Why isn't it possible all the ensembles,
These impossible getups, are somehow designer
Commemoratives of you, the lovelier for being
The less real and seldom difficult to desire.
Afternoons, they come on as billboards until
Who covets them can hardly know his state, can feel
His stately heart cut loose and lose its balance
As item hard after item spreads
Provocation to those preceding and forward
To these beyond: it's how temptation heats up
By increment to make the last also the least
Resistible—and here it is, securely indifferent
While surely aimed to please. Check it out; the tags
Are snapping and the offer is made in style.

SUMMER

Everywhere things have been taking place
Visibly, filling vacancies as if these
Were where they accurately belonged.
Likewise with us, it is no isolated longing
We are called on to endure, encouraged
By the loose joints of each expanding afternoon,
This season we never could have made
Save for the hours that buckle and gully
Beside us with desire. Headlong as it seems,
Our momentum is still an adjunct
Of the year and the territory we cover
Is legitimately ours, as when yellow rocket
Retakes an empty field. What's to decide?
The invisible volume of richness within our grasp
Is unfathomable unless we retrieve it
In peculiar experience: a day at the beach,
A trip to the country, a morning that starts
With the loudest cardinal we ever heard.
And though these moments will ripen by themselves
We are not likely to be surprised
If they turn up heaped together one day
Like a pail of raspberries ready to be cleaned,
In total no fuller and no less than the space
That was exactly available at the time.
It's enough to occupy dimensions

As we come to them, the handsome couple
Just now appearing at the door,
And how we measure their eventual reach
We can wait for time to tell. Today though,
Today crowds the branches in busy readiness,
The abundant minutes are plentiful all around,
And immediately as the afternoon begins
The wind arrives
With the flutter of something really happening.

GREAT FENNVILLE SWAMP

The thing about the Great Fennville Swamp is your father
Going through it in his canoe, not what that signifies
But what it does, the limp algae wake that would be made,
The sluggish disturbance in the pointillistic skin he'd
Paddle through. The thing about the Great Fennville Swamp
Is approaching it on your own in your own canoe, young
With discovery, enough peanut butter provisions close
At hand, and the river's touching momentum as if it were
A stand-in for your guide. The thing about the Fennville
Swamp is, when you enter it, its bleaching humidities
Have begun: minerals, sleek as minks, slip through the
Surface to dissolve in accumulating beds of peat and muck.
The thing about this factor of the swamp is it's a factory,
Thick with feedstocks, to reduce raw cat-tails and the
Separating pulp of dead jack pines—a refinery to crack
The uncouth molecules in its patient soak. The thing is,
With a swamp you're between a dying lake and still-emerging
Land, the end product sinks to the bottom and there's no
Place for certain where the original processing leaves off
Just as the latest technologies began. The thing about a
Swamp in this state is the place it occupies in time: the
First settlers passed the whole territory for fear of fever
And water moccasins, and, despite the irreversible success
Of immigration when it came, those who remember still warn
You of the worst: all Michigan to be a swamp someday.

The thing about a swamp is where it is, and if it takes
A lot of getting to. The thing is, what does it provide—
Cat-tails, pussy willows, bright with poison sumac at its
Side? The thing is, if you take the Fennville Swamp, muskrats
Are possible, bones of a mastodon, mud herons standing on
One leg, but no archaeological trinkets here: even Indians
Seem to avoid the swamps, which has to account for the lack
Of an Indian name. The thing about the Great Fennville Swamp
Then is its name (the Swampville Swamp), with even an extra
N to secure foreigners "fen" and "ville." The thing about
That is the way it sounds. The thing about sounds is the way
The swamp sounds at night, a blank tape hissing with too
Much gain, and nothing but background in the background you
Can hear. The thing about the Great Fennville Swamp is that
It's always taking place, each hummock of reeds gone under,
Each brown pine needle on the stagnant bays, the exhausted
Delicate dead mosquito shells, inexhaustibly decomposed.
The thing about the Great Fennville Swamp is when you near
The edge of it at night, when you see the dim outline of
Its glacial ridge; the thing is when you leave the trapped
Canoe, when the treacherous muck starts turning into slick
Hard land, when you finally hit hard land, you run,
Reach the sweet hogback and in the clear cold dark begin
To contemplate the lonely walk back home on solid ground.

IN MEMORY OF MY COUNTRY

As the land lifts
The weather begins at once to wear it down:
Its ridges lose their minerals in the rain,
Its valleys open in wide parallels. The hills
Sink of their own weight into plains, the plains
Sag into rivers of their own debris, and features
Hard as rocks will be transformed
To clouds of dust that drip out of the sky.
It is the land, as it appears,
That tells the world of time: conglomerate,
So fiercely made to pass through day and night,
Heaped up and gullied and borne away.
The falls cut upstream every year, the delta
Spreads, the breakers sort the sands
With no mistake. There is no place on earth
Hidden from earth's patient spin: the stumps
Of mountains turn in the same custody
As the worn plateau over which they rise.
Hard as granite, the weather levels the record
Of the toughest past whose moments unfasten
In confusion with the active land.

WHITEOUT

Now we account for movement when we can't:
The plane tree peeled to white—the whiter sky—
The fuselage borne in winter, air or trial.
Is it Bulova where the departure ramp draws near?
Hands hide in their awnings, but the notes are up
And walking in the aisle. I hold you
When nobody lives in another's world, those millions.
What references can we give, which ones request?
The baggage is trembling in the cold, long distance,
And everything comes from Texas in small amounts.
The future is hardly big enough for the past
Though we stoop into rush hour
Which will have to do. The key goes shining for the lock,
The garage door down behind in the white dark.

THE WINTER HOUSE

At last I am in for the sure season: sage,
Lovage, tarragon are dried and hung in easy reach,
Tomatoes reduced to a manageable puree, a waste
Of apple, pear, and peach consolidated in labeled
Jars, already gathering dust on the basement shelves.
The light, longer along the ground than it is tall,
Doesn't surround me anymore but seems independent
From the earth, an element of day and not the definition
Of it. The active scenery falls away. Sounds
Skip long distances as if they were bouncing on
A sparer curvature. Only a few sparrows, tenacious
As little milkweed pods, cling to their dry footing
In level November air. Otherwise, ripe things
Have lessened their hold, gone to seed, disappeared,
And in the middle of this remoteness I am alone.
But there is something more to look at, after all,
For just as every effect produces an equal and maybe
Opposite effect, in the seasons there is a kind of law
Of conservation of fullness and vision that takes over
And as things disappear they leave behind the clear
Outline of the immensities they occupied, their cool
Horizons, the long months I need to orient myself
To them. The pale certainties are inescapable:
The outside light contracts, the inside one expands

Out of necessity from this zero center, and all
I have to do is look out the cold window to see
Its idiosyncratic crystals grow, crinkling,
In every direction over the frozen ground.

REPLEVIN

If the beginning of love
Is loss, possessing it
In places where you know
It can be seen, then
The reason for love is
Retrieval, arranging it
To fit the space where
It always might have been.
If the manner of love
Is displaying it, faithful
As if belonging were,
Then the assumption of love
Is correcting it, rightful
Proportions rightfully
To restore. If the effect
Of love is regaining it,
In greetings as over
Distances overcome,
Then the source of love
Is remembering it, the
Illusion of love is
Reshaping it, and the life
Of love is embracing
Its perpetual
Unattainable selves.

COVENANT

To live with me and be
My love, proposing it
As if all the pleasures
Came to the same test,
Invites the love from living
In for life, deposing it
With an innocent lively
Tension of intent. And
To live with me *or* be
My love, selecting it
As if without the other's
Commerce the one could live,
Secures the life from loving
In live death, protecting it
With a deadly living
Waste of discontent. But
To love with me and live
My love, engaging it
One from the other neither
Leaving off, is to love
In the life of division
And live in loving it,
Where if loving only lives
It dies
But if living only will love
Then loving will live.

TROVER

If the leaning of love
Is to learn, investing it
In acts that you intend
For their effect, then
The effort of love is
Example, addressing it
In practices
Exact to each respect.
If the method of love
Is rehearsing it, faithful
As if a performance were,
Then the tension of love
Is attending it, skillful
Ambitions skillfully
Played for more. If the motive
Of love's reproducing it
In habit come close as
Habit can ever come,
Then the turn of love
Is resembling it, the
Trial of love is
Revealing it, and the fate
Of love is in facing
Its eventual
Duplicate done.

THE ONE WHO

CROSSED THE HUDSON

Listen, it was not what he wanted
Though the approach took up his life for years
So fitly reverse of what we had supposed
We might have taken out a policy on the result,
It was that predictable. Like a tunnel at rush hour,
I can tell you he hardly had a choice. Naturally,
He wasn't quick to it at first, preferring to linger
In our direction through the wide suburbs
And little college towns where the lift and trim of things
Would be less surprised than he knew it ought to be. But look,
He liked it there, having seen the aprons between us,
Lucent, rigged with refineries
And the bluest wires to tumble out of our streets about him
Or feed back into them—aprons of tank farms
And fields of stars cracking. Everywhere
There was nowhere to negotiate a stop, bladder screaming,
Tires steaming toward us and turned to our devices. Here
To have supper as one of us, to enter
Without blip or trace marking the point of departure
From the norm—can you see how this explains his hanging fire
So far from what anyone had supposed though close
As the reverse of it? "It was done for a better view
Of the bank he loved." As if one needed to explain

His descent via tollbooth or even, prior,
The prelude at Nessie's Cottage Bar
Rapt in the dalliance of a clock whose letters
NEW BRUNSWICK (all art deco twelve of them)
Replaced twelve Roman numerals. How the grand sonnerie
Of delay would come to treasure him, would accelerate
Four times an hour the B, the R, the K—*brake*
Break—how, with neither claim nor clarity, would trail
Along to sound first "Halt" and then "Escape"
While he led his progress nevertheless to—what?—
What we were waiting for. No opening:
Ramp, bridge, or lane will hug him in, *Phragmites*
Tight to his fenders and wide in the wake of him
When, over the rickety skyway, down the road,
Is revealed in front of night this bright conditional,
Our rise and fall,
The breath of blue movies, the bounce and toss
Of the chemical mattress for which—precisely when was it?—
We traded in the sky. Deeper than fossils,
Fuller than coal is formed, I tell you we've done it again
And he is ours. Time enough to strike the medal.
For now let's have him up and get acquainted
(Hello, injured and curious) over that overdue meal.

IN DEFENSE OF

ELLIS HOLLOW CREEK

Rather than innocence, I recognize
The claim of knowledge abandoned at its source,
Learned fresh with happening and fit to the universe
Though small, and exclusive as things are where they grow
Exact. In their surroundings one gets to know
The lively specificity of things (the arrowhead
Half out of the water and a third in bloom) as naturally
Arranged to habitat as the succession of boneset,
Snakeroot and Joe-Pye weed that proceeds from the creek
Straight to the back porch door. After learning the
First one, they each seem silent with uses in a way,
Coiled like the seed of touch-me-nots to be released
In season according to the experience at hand:
Some Indian remedy known three hundred years ago
For afflictions that never required *Mayflower* transport
After all. Yes, growing up is like being a colonist
And it's nice to know about new worlds when young,
That arrowhead is duck potato and you could live
Through winter stealing it from the muskrat storage
Bins, but taxonomies of wonder dry at an early age,
One stops walking barefoot in the creek and learns
To drive, and the starch of childhood gets buried
Life by life not when it's useless but only when

It is no longer used. Like legal age or the Revolution,
Lifelike experience has come to be acquired as
A function of cutoff points in time, a disposition
Toward divorce that has made short work of yesterday.
Some of the farms around have been next to deserted
Since the Civil War. Their news arrives in the evening:
Information about the world that wasn't gathered from
The world. Far from innocence, what's left untended
Is what took years of living in one spot to learn
(The map turtle on his rock, the kingfisher
Buzzing the creek along her altitude): a marginal joy
Proceeding as common sense, age to commemorate
Its attentive childhood the way the life of a creek
Is measured in distance not in time,
As the place I grew up could be the one I live.

PART FIVE

GUNPOWDER MORNING

IN A GRAY ROOM

Everything turns up in me in time
As a month will ride the refrigerator door
For months into winter, heading home. The furnace,
Which is nearly too close for comfort when it comes on,
Moves secrets truer than functions inside the room
By every one of which I'm to be warned and drawn,
And though this is impossible because none is there
Gradually they lay up their own temper anyhow
As if to prove, "Meantime, this is the way rest is:
On a siding an empty flatcar will fill with snow."
For a person, it gets to be a matter of concern
Being the transport of too many arguments not your own
And under a season patiently endured (piling up,
Melting away, piling up and melting away)
It's natural to envy the pitch of pure integrity,
How it would be living under that roof—
The weight of the climate slipped from the eaves
Along with the snow. Not to feel the weather,
How would that feel? To be tuned to a shape
Long since assumed, sure, single, *in from the wind.*
There are people like this, steep with intent
And valid as of that entry long ago. Each time
They are more engagingly unreal, these precious others

Who persist unrearranged, unregistering. Still,
To be in is to miss the way the day went
And this is so: the "as ifness" of the world is real,
Productive, wherever it comes from can't be ignored
Though it may work against the solidest masonry,
The oldest of fieldstone farmhouse walls. The manner
Of meaning is its drift from whatever it means with,
The same as a snowdrift elaborates wind
Out of obstacles to the wind, being altered daily
To be annually kept true. Not to be of that climate
Though, how would that be? An accurate morning
Unintervened, a color alike indoors as out,
And the sound of somebody spinning their tires
Neither to come for me nor as if to go.

IN THE FALL WHEN
IT'S TIME TO LEAVE

FOR FRANK POLACH

When your mind is on the move (it is fall,
You are moving away) it meets many familiar things
It does and it doesn't recognize for the first time.
Common encounters (the toothbrush mistakenly shared)
Add up to direction as certain as "follow the dotted
Line" and portents too good to be true (sycamores,
Or were they London planes?) show up in number
And increasing speed. It's one of those times
When everything has to happen fast, one lease
Run out and the new one yet to sign, a time
That could even make up for all those years
Of "seek and ye shall find" as the ordinary,
Though not what you were looking for, turns
Like the leaves into discovery before your eyes.
It is the end of summer though it's a funny way
To end it—off balance in a spread of goldenrod,
A figure in the near distance of a Dash landscape
Not quite at home with movement but likely
To continue on. Two kinds of goldenrod as every year,
One scented and the other "un," except for you
It's a fresh distinction to take the "who cares?"

79

Out of your attitude and send you walking
Around mooning as if you'd never seen a weed before.
This morning before the train comes the importance
Of the world reveals itself, immodest as the play
Of "pilgrim" light and almost tangible, more insistent
And approaching than the hour. One after another,
Incidents of wind pile up against the house
So that you start trying to keep track of them,
Each more significant than the last because
Their corroborating number proves it's fall.
In times of transition (and fall is always
One of those) you are a sitting duck for signs
And maybe you didn't encourage them, but when
They appear on schedule at least you are prepared
Which is something you ought to think about.
It's the same light, you know, on the crowded
Weedstems and the dusty windows of the waiting car.
It only feels like leaving; you take the train
Because it's going to get someplace.
The signs are everywhere, as clear as day.

BLUE POLES

What we bring back is the sense of the size of it,
Potential as something permanent is, the way a road map
Of even the oldest state suggests in its tangled details
The extent of a country in which topography and settlement
Interrupt only at random into a personal view. Everything,
Having been discovered, is remembered bit by bit in singular
Unforgetting dreams. Deep in the interior of Brazil
We hear of an unnamed river a thousand kilometers long
And the surveyors are finally getting there late this year.
On our own continent, it took La Salle and Lewis & Clark
To retrieve in meticulous renderings an arroyo here,
An opening there, but from a distance we see at one time
The expeditionary surface whole and not the outrageous mile
On every mile their canoes and pack horses have achieved.
Tedious and however unimportant, these are the essential
Known unknowns in a tight terrain. Inevitably,
As we fill in where the explorations went, we retrace
First steps in undirected time unerringly down the same
Erratic riverbeds, between identical steep canyon walls
As bright with the events of their formation as if
There were no secret past. Seeming outside experience,
Affixed like lichens or embedded like a point of quartz,
They are instead the particulars surrounding present
Consciousness with its ever-active sense of scale.
Along the fierce faults of an igneous history

They are thrust free and fused in any order to betray
By their eidetic mass the tensions as well as materials
Which are released in them. Serene and adamantly enlarged,
Seismic totems arranged at the rim of day, they advance
On the waking extent of the world, what it knew.

SAGG BEACH

It's usual walking to the beach
And just this way. The route so naturally accustomed
Forms itself from us and just as naturally
With others here will change. We move among
The objects that we choose, this coat that fits,
This pebble that you love because it's blue,
And these accumulating weight will bring us home.
Yes, childhood's one of nature's hardest things:
No worse than the ocean though, and beautiful at the edge
It meets and leaves. A thousand surfaces
And each might have been exactly else,
As sure as any raw material, but comes to us
Shined as it is, to be. The passengers in your painting
Of the train rest in the faces that they wear—
Anonymous with travel, arrived at honestly? Should we
Count the eddies that brought them to their seats
The back and forth of moments paying fare,
Currents guilty with good-byes or devious to avoid
The pleading obstacles? Their heads are round or long
Accordingly, but when they bump against the windows:
Personal fact. Not one of them who couldn't be happier,
Yet each one sunk in his compartment as a stone,
The gem of a little history not to be undone. In them
The present seems a firm result, in us the endless shame
Of a model manufacture that went wrong. We dream

On our potential as if nothing had happened since,
On our behavior as if it could be melted and recast,
As if we were each the parents of our specifications
And not their child. It's an anxious excursion,
Red-penciling your infancy. Believe me,
Since you are here with us, and though the experience
Of your design was vast and cruel, each one of us
Can see your shape and envy you. The form you have
Is just as you are, real, and when you shine
It is with this delivered fact.

FELIX CULPA RETURNS

FROM FRANCE

SPEAKER

As the fact is too difficult to forgive
It seems unnatural to resume, lopsided
To come in straight off the street this way
With another diurnal thesis for the file.
Each new description works its prejudice
Until things that seemed by nature to anticipate,
Books on the shelf, maps of green counties
To vacation in, are bent to perform
Instead a prior restraint. There's nothing
So quick as the opening moment and nothing
More quickly betrayed to pride, that veteran
Lobby in favor of history. By formula,
Futures depreciate thus: the styles
Corrode the systems on which they are hung
And even commemoration will add offense.
In the progression of thought, word, deed,
The styles insulate knowledge from the self,
Self from action, action from the common good
Whose bull's-eye present unzipped is
Never seen and never to be seen again—
All we have to go on being the clue,

Clumsier than what was, of what was is.
Outside this pileup it's impossible
To behave; though given it one fashion
Nimble personals, a skip down the shoulder,
A picnic in the grassy median, none
Is so agile he or she outstep
The conglomerate precedent of the age,
The stare decisis in our blind-as-justice
Verb, to be. We started where?—pledged
To the logical consequence of the arts
And, prepared for ambition, preparing
Ambition's tools. So the issue has settled
As was said: those split from the earth,
With but the bodies and rumor of others
To labor on, are bringing their harvest home—
A wronged Thanksgiving of product and
Caprice, all in a steamy, over-urban
Stew. It makes the story one came to tell
Untellable, as much an accident
As population and equally unacceptable.

ROLL FILM

A man who boards a plane and does not fly.
An eye that measures him but does not spy.
A start the man can leave and not deny.

SPEAKER

Life without thought of it
There like Louisiana to accede; my claim
Went with the sun's, ahead of time. Impossible,
But to begin with here was all the world
And where to choose fell level on each field
Of alfalfa (for nitrogen) or, in rotation,
Corn. To plant was natural, sped by machinery
Constant in repair: plow, disk, drag, cultivate
And spray. The second cutting waited on
The first, a little early but more often late,
And sometimes we were managing a third: mow,
Rake (to rake in triangles was fun),
Then bale to beat the rain the night before,
The tractor stiff to its business, windrows
Arched, and once the power take-off is engaged
There's nothing to stop the flywheel but the dew.
Load, stack, unload and stack: you work your ass off
Doing what you can and if the stuff gets wet
The cows won't like it but they won't know why;
In ruminants I've never seen reproach. Dominion
Was the name for custody of water cups
And gutters, to keep them clean. Dominion over
The compressor and the milkers the compressor runs,
Over stanchions and the swallows that nest above
The stanchions and over barn cats underfooting it
To be fed. Dominion over dry ice bitching in the tub,

Over semen thawed, over heifers showing their first signs
Of heat. Dominion of mastitis and the fear of Bang's,
Of sticky whitewash and of culling from
A hundred head that trust you and forgive
Your fixed authority, their little choice. Unanimous,
Your chores are moved along without regret.
The weather turns, it turns on everyone, and school
Lets out on time to pick the corn. In August
The stars began to fall and if there was evil
Then there was, but it was lost in opportunity.

ROLL FILM

Jefferson coming home is wiser,
Wiser than we, to be followed
By much French furniture.
In his brain, deeply folded,
The continents fit and part again.

SPEAKER

A proper confusion. The interface
Of morality and style's a natural,
Which explains why the issue now
Is less development and more of what
To recognize. With space enough

No behavior was out of bounds, meaning
One gets homesick for the horizon first,
For big sky and for free-soil virtue
Under it, for unlimited solar access
Under the principle "one man, one sun,"
For the right to raise livestock,
Rolling stock, common stock—all
In anticipation of fair return:
A correct life and correctly earned.
But if this privilege cannot be
Maintained, the trick is to locate
With agility and even grace—in the
Least differentiated state there's a
Last-ditch enclave to be found, a loft
A mother couldn't love, waiting on you
To be picture-perfect as showplace
And as personal preserve. This
Is the practice one learns to undertake:
To be spry in the interest of coaxing
Your due is just apportionment
With examples clear and not unscrupulous.
Aren't waters from the land of the watersheds
Flown to the city where all of the watertowers
Are on their nests? Now in such infra-
Structure of course are social costs
But places as well where, as a citizen,
You drink for free and no one assembles
To picket or object, the system having

Been built for you. No matter that "you"
Were intended in the abstract; your tap
On these works fulfills their intent
To the glory of those who proposed them
And of their engineers. Some years
There's more of a birthright and some years
Less, but with or without your birth
The needle would register and therefore
Isn't measuring you. The curve it describes,
From philanthropy to larceny, is wealth:
One basks or squirms in it but, as with
Temperature, is not responsible. One lives
As one has been endowed, except one goes on
Living and here is where the fun comes in
Because everyone has an out in everyone else,
The chance to be witnessed behaving as he
Or she behaves—and if this is the entree
Of guilty life, well, welcome to it,
Guilty of wanting to save the world
All in its presently visible self.

CHELSEA SQUARE

There are these remnants of what was local
And planned-for in our lives, deep doorways
Lingering, Greek details shut away in shadow
And brownstone in truncated strata
Hugging the island as if this were the afternoon
It was finally going to throw them off.
In the aggravated geology of the city there are
Whole neighborhoods having their ups and downs,
The thunderous bedrock erupts into planar bluffs
That split and glow, and somewhere around four
On chill afternoons it seems the prodigious schist
En masse from river to river will lift the city
On mica cliffs, tunnels and bridges dangling,
And sleek chips of isinglass fall away to sparkle
All at once above the surface, one at a time.
How long has it been since glacial assurances
Backed off to leave this split in the terminal
Moraine through which the ocean rushed to maroon us
Among its estuaries and tidal straits? Right now
The gulls rise like a thousand magnesium fires
Among the incandescent sky-high towers. We have
Touched the sun, if only with the horizon,
And already in the cold streets night fills
The formidable aftermath. Here and there

At different levels around us the separate lights
Appear, tiny as campfires on a distant hill.
Out of reach across the river, dark and inevitable,
The gathering mainland is beginning to breathe.

WHEN SPRING COMES FIRST

TO WEST 21ST STREET

The day we discovered the world
Was the day it had also been there all the time,
Furious to be documented in the seasons which grow on us
So unnoticeably. At Montauk the lighthouse again
Is closer to the sea and above Dyckman Street
The nets have been spread to catch the running shad,
Fewer though not less vigorous than they used to be.
In the bookstores even the lichens are said
To be in danger now (the lichens, think of that)
But in the city we've got the sparrows going at it
Flagrante delicto before our eyes, apparently
Unembarrassed by DDT. It must be spring
And the blood badgering underneath the skin
Is one of the spring ephemerals perking up
Before the overpowering shade of summer does it in.
Considering its circumstance, the smell of sweet bay
In the Bronx is close to sickening in sentiment:
What have we done? Is it true the English
Could have called Long Island as they did, Eden?
Anyway, if the seas keep warming up it will all be gone
And it may be our sense of this that unlocks the day,
Bringing trout lilies and marsh marigolds into mind
As the last of the concerts are letting out uptown,

And this that brings eight hundred to watch the egrets
In Jamaica Bay (one ten-thousandth of a percent:
Viewed thus, "population per capita" is really small).
Stolen, our love of the world
Must be stolen from the world the way hepaticas
Steal light from the climax forest
Where alone they are able to grow. Too much with us
And too soon, the world extends its canopy
To alter the feel as well as color of the air.
How much time we have is hard to say
But, swift as the camera's shutter when it flowers,
That's how swift we're going to have to be
As the bloom of swamp maples reddens into the past
Just like the sun. The speed of the seasons
And their slant remain untouched and unidentified
Until the beauty of something beautiful makes the day.

COLOR PEAK WEEKEND

Things have moved closer together again. Every red
In the spectrum rankles one *Acer rubrum* branch: rose,
Copper, scarlet, rose, tipping each other red for red.
Alone, which of them wouldn't be simply red?
So much is pressed in its sufficient scale, fired
By what seem opposites but aren't. The kames, warmed up
Through evening, are cool green. The colder kettles
Are burning maple red. If Wyman (*Trees for American Gardens*)
Could know it, he'd rest his theory in Mount Hope: sugar
And tannin trapped by frost, a boil of waste, a stew
(Jambalaya)—what makes things come together when they fall?
Or when they come up again, for that matter? The children
Are at the door for caramels, apples, dressed in sheets.
They are ghostly but full of luminous spark, their own.
Or is it shared, passed around like the gas off the marshes
At night? Like the haystacks of Martin Johnson Heade,
What would one of them be alone? Trick or treat: the haystacks
Are at the door. Time (no time) to answer. A student
Has arrived in town, "the perfect replacement," you said,
"For So-and-so, right down to his accent, right down
To his place of birth." But of course he isn't. So-and-so
Is gone, a graduate to an income (how do we say it now?)
Upscale. Well, we have the new one for four years,
To teach him—of all things—what we teach them:
Difference. A pumpkin looks much like a squash, but isn't.

Because a goldfinch fades as the goldenrods fade
You cannot assume they are the same. Though each is
Pale sumac, a cardinal (female) is not a pin oak leaf.
How can we tend such knowledge, flung as it is in the face
Of things? This week, wasn't Monday on Monday again?
Next week, won't we elect a president? No matter
How you define it, when you sit down to the piano
You can't move middle C. The sun is the center of seasons
And they are one, though fired within by opposites, one
With the year the sun makes. And if the sun
Is not the center of the universe it will still be found
The sun belongs, and the seasons around it belong,
And the students who fill with tannin belong: rose,
Copper, scarlet, rose, tipping each other red for red.
Alone, what isn't the universe? Don't pages
Turn in the hymnal, *Duke Street, Nun Danket,*
Old Hundred Twenty-Fourth, each with its own first line
Much like the rest? The Puerto Rican kids dress up
As the Druid dead. Salt hay is mown in the marshes
And the cardinals turn to the feeder, male as sumac,
Female as a fallen pin oak leaf. The sharps
Are bunched up on the keyboard looking like flats
Though with practice they separate.

THERE IS NO REAL PEACE

IN THE WORLD

The fact of life is it's no life-or-death matter,
Which is supposed to make it easier to choose. People die,
For sure, and that's a personal apocalypse for them
And a revision of heaven and earth for those "left
To follow after" (as your great-grandfather's obituary would say)
So that a few are always being rearranged on maps
Redrawn by family accident or folly, like separate Europes
After their awful wars. War isn't the easiest metaphor
To go by though, nor, here's the point, is it reliable
Since all the individual hells added up remain exactly
Individual, and whether they blaze like Berlin or not
Are kept in those unassailable bunkers, Born and Died,
Passed in and out of this world, the whole world minus one,
Which never felt the flames nor ever knew. No,
No sooner has one perished than the rest survive,
Which ought to be proof that yes-or-no options aren't final
As they seem to be, except for the problem that the survivor
In our time includes memories out of all proportion to
The experience ahead of him and is intent on living up to them,
On Germany where there's only Idaho. It's inescapable
How history has targeted the tiniest, safest life
With the knowledge that chance and power, unmitigated,
Are always impending out of the godless distance toward it

The way there is always a comet impending toward the earth
And it's only a question now of how close and when,
A recombinant message which has breached the world
And altered the code so thoroughly that issues graceful once
As travel or turning the calendar beget features of flight,
Contortion and alarm instead. If it's in the inheritance
It's in the life, and why should it be disregarded
Because the evidence, the rock-hard impact,
Is still to occur? By then it would be too late
For the genius of worry is to duck the Gotterdammerungs
That might establish its validity, to live close enough
To the border to get away and know where to do it
(Minnesota, Montana, never Niagara Falls), to have
Plenty of birth certificates on hand, a respectable lawyer
And a self-sufficient farm tucked into an unknown corner
Of that same Idaho. But the truth is, as I said, to date
It's only Idaho, a kind of demilitarized zone at most
Where life is interchangeable with the regrets expressed
When it is over, nothing to touch off the silos for.
There's grain in the hopper and wives sweet with biphenyls
Under the skin, or else fatigue—who knows for sure? The cows
Are freshening off schedule again. There is nothing to fear.

THE ASTROPASTORALS

ONCE THE SOLE PROVINCE

of genius here at home,
Was it this, our idea of access to a larger world
That invented the world itself (first, second,
Third), past accuracy we are bound to inhabit now
As targets, positioned in a trillionth
Of the smallest measuring—microresults
Made in the least, most unimaginable chronology?
No more time-outs. For we are either ready or
We must be ready or not, an expensive mix
Of life-based chemistry perpetually on the verge
Of going to heaven in a vapor, and almost making it,
Almost, except there's that one true destiny
Incontestably driving down on us,
The finally collapsible ones,
Who are lumped in a uniform density at last,
At last coherent to desire. It is a density
Greater than the sun's.

But Day,
There must be some other reference,
Which is why you so nervously dwell on us,
On earth which keeps turning, embarrassed, from the light:
Indiscriminate shine on Shiite, Methodist, Hun,
And pump of excitability. Dissatisfied,
As all things are on earth,

Is there anything earthly that can't be made to rise,
Emit disciples, the collimated and the laser lean?
They march to you, old outside agitator,
While you who pump the world with promises
Are simply not to believed. All those diversions,
The years and decades, the manifold span of life
—These were the dialectic of a fold
Formed out of almost nothingness, a fold of hours
In a space where the "hour" is eccentricity. So
Pity the day, beyond which we can see,
For if time is distance then distance must be life
And who is there on earth who will not go
In answer to its call? Call this
The aim of every reverence:
That outside ourselves there be a scale more vast,
Time free of whimsy, an endless unbended reach
In which to recollect our planet, our hours, and ourselves.

A reductionism that makes the world
complex, a truth that simply nothing
can explain, is how events curled
up in space when seen are scattering.

DOG STAR SALE

Now the universe wants to be known
For itself, isn't that why we're here
Popped out on this terrace the color of stars
The red ones like gentrified brick

Lucky for us
It takes money to even imagine
Such things and this, for parsecs around,
Is the one place where money is made
Though not everyone has it, not even here

The burden is on those who do
Which we freely take up
Our volitional duty to curate the spheres
After how many misfired suns
And misapplied genes
How many millions fed to despair
Before we were brought to the task
Thankless, that cannot be failed

Just to think of it
Sometimes engenders a chill
So thorough the planet's own breath
Will draw back on its bones

And there in that vault sucked by fear
One has shivered at twinkles of something
Not normally shown

It explains the wide pupils
And why I protect them
When doing so keeps me from you
All involved on the earth with your chores of pollution
And likely never to pause
Let alone practice what we
Observe: as far as you touch
Other worlds, that much you save yours

SALE II

So the promotionals
Get harder to resist this way
And ditto the things
They advertise. All could be mine
Just for ditching this live indecision
Some tend to call
As if they knew what to compare it to
Life on the earth

Let them not count me out
Let me read their desires to ignition
And then let me burn
Intensely as they burn
In faith like a prairie fire. Don't
Let me retire too soon from the mission
To light out for anywhere just as we are
To settle our plan for salvation
On the first spinning rock of the first
Rock-surrounded dim star. O pilgrims
And real-estate shock troops
Look who's for hire

THEME PARK

Too much of a subject can interfere,
Be a drag, so subvert the procedure to which it refers
That the wisest course is to visit it just for fun,
Have fun, and make a clean getaway—wisdom
Already shed in the shiver of pilgrim foot
On the longed-for soil. Truly no one ahead,
Until this is where our lives become sweet and true,
Begun on the clumpy green with its circle of flowers,
Its flagpole and founders' memorial, map
Of self-guided tours, viewing sites, trail.
And farther, more deeply recessed and peacefuller
Still, the substantive structures themselves
Are seen meeting their needs in scale: shops,
Ammo dumps, taverns, and houses of prayer. But
Who could be sure of a tenure except in this world,
Fair between the river and the sea?—where the birds
And the natives, so enthused by our coming,
Run back and forth like children on the shore.

TRUE SOLAR HOLIDAY

Out of the whim of data,
Out of binary contests driven and stored,
By the law of large numbers and subject to that law
Which in time will correct us like an event,
And from bounce and toss of things that aren't even things
I've determined the trend I call "you" and know you are real,
Your unwillingness to appear
In all but the least likely worlds, as in this world
Here. In spite of excursions, despite my expenditures
Ever more anxiously matrixed, ever baroque,
I can prove we have met and I've proved we can do it again
By each error I make where otherwise one couldn't be
Because only an actual randomness
Never admits a mistake. It's for your sake,
Then, *though the stars get lost from the bottle,*
Though the bottle unwind, if I linger around in the wrong
Ringing up details, pixel by high bit by bit,
In hopes of you not as integer but at least as the sum
Of all my near misses, divisible
Once there is time to an average that poses you perfectly
Like a surprise, unaccidentally credible
Perfectly like a surprise. Am I really too patient,
When this is the only program from which you derive?
Not if you knew how beautiful you will be,
How important it is your discovery dawn on me,

How as long as I keep my attention trained
Then finally the days
Will bow every morning in your direction as they do to the sun
That hosannas upon that horizon
Of which I am witness and not the one farther on
—Set to let me elect you as though there were no other choice,
Choice made like temperature, trend I can actually feel.

Under the rim of maybe
Back on the edge of regret
Around the corner from should have
Down the street from forget
Out on a limb with willing
Too far gone to remark
Close to the tip of almost
Up slip creek in the dark

TO THE LIGHT FANTASTIC

Nor are the fashions always fickle
Or imposed, but may occur as breakthroughs
In tandem with our need for them, the need
They were orbiting unnoticed all that time.
Invented, these burst upon a world agog
With its own gravity, a world of matter
Where the trade is energy, a world
Whose minds in many private laboratories
May suddenly wave an identical flag
In each of them, the report of which
Thrills all the media: a century
Begins—begins because it discovered

The rights of man, or unearthed light.
And ours? if it isn't breaking on the scene,
Must be begun somewhere in prototype,
Be protected by patents, nourished
In the flush of R & D. Somewhere,
Already in line with theory, where
The deracinated secrets reel by,
Where the cameras gaze on their unlikely provenance . . .

All the satellites scattered in heaven
Nod, until by laws of motion
That consortium is stirred whose teams

Reciprocate their codes from many
Terminals, knowing, the moment more
Come online than ever before, inertia
Is undone: enlightenment—does it
Enter as light with the speed of light
To delineate all this earth (emirate,
Nation, principality) whose arrangement
Is finally making its debut, got up
In a possible planet, as was made?

CONNECTICUT

So much motion is love.
Though sometimes it's also exile
Or the "bent of our spirits to remove"
Nearer their venue of desire, still motion
Is love, pressed forward in hopes of
Never being left behind and never having, meanwhile,
Gone too far: a dilemma
Terribly settled here first by those, outdistanced
Otherwise, who dispelled all else before them,
Naming it New World. Fierce state of

Forgetfulness!—if ever your ancient affections
Offer a fight, if writ or rebellion
Restore them to power or redress of letters

Jimmy them free, then let me recall but one
Mere rebel more whose love you might move on to be.

THE PAYS D'EN HAUT SUBLIME

FOR BRIAN WALKER

The fables were always upcountry, but
The sublime
Understood in its practical sense as
This map of vista and refuge that slides into mind
Whenever you simply are looking
Has to be here: its precincts
So free of protection, freely desired,
And reached by that hard-driving warpath
Where each vote was personal, something you feel,
Cut time. The fashions
Are always downriver, not the sublime.
It lingers the unlicensed wealth
Due to any inhabitant, some,
Who would hurry its data into an ardent shape
As if life were a sensate
Cartography. So it could seem
In this land where the maps all lie flat
Until, trying one on,
You proceed via graphic new molt as your whole country
Walking—in whose indefensible habits
Let me come too, though the facts
Turn to fables themselves, strike back and run.

ASTROPASTORAL

As much as the image of you, I have seen
You again, live, as in live indecision you brighten
The limbs of an earth that so earnestly turns
To reflect you, the sky's brightest body
And last best beacon for those who are everywhere
Coded in spirals and want to unbend,
Who bear in the dark turned toward you
This message they have to deliver even to live,
To linger in real time before you, to meet or to
Blow you away—and yes I have seen you receive them
But you are not there. Though I've tried to ignore you,
Go solo, light out beyond you,
I have seen you on every horizon, how you are stored
And encouraged and brought to the brim
Until the round bounds of one planet could not hold you in
But were ready to set near space ringing
As if from the ranking capacitor outside the sun.
I have seen you discharged, and then how you swell
Toward heaven and how you return, transmitting the fun
Of the firmament, all of it yours. And these things
Have happened, only you are not there.
At night in the opposite high-rise I'd see how you glow,
And in the adjacent one too, the same would-be blue,
And I've looked on the glow in the waters

Around the reactor, that also blue, how
Whatever would match your expression you
Wouldn't be there. I have seen the impressions you leave
At the margin of error in exit polls, monitored polls
That you never entered—I can tell what I see:
Saw you vote with your feet and hit the ground running,
Kiss the ground, rescued, and (*this wasn't a drill*)
Saw you fall to your knees on the ground
By the body of your friend on the ground
And though these fall beside you like gantries, it is
You who are rising above them and you are not there.
Like a rocket in winter, I have been there to see you
Logged in as a guest among stars—only you,
Though you're lovely to look at, expensive to own,
And though in demand without letup, you are not there.

Time: when not to come undone
is, no, not slavery. Happiness
defines the accommodation
that hides the quark from us.

REFUGE

The mitigation remembers the mischief,
And nothing's repaired except to engender it
Different. All things are wild
In the service of objects toward which they verge
—Each amendment is wild, and the touch
On the refuse truck wheel tears up Valley Brook
Road. We were here for the view, and in that
We are a success because this is our scene:
Tracks, turnpike, a pipeline, the landfill,
Amenities meant for the wildlife in
The error-prone acreage between. No habitat
Scans like a wasteland, but by what unmistakable
Eye? The truck stirs the mice, the hawk
Heart stirs, and rodents in motion resolve
In fast-focus foveae. Life lifts from, it
Harries the ground, and the study a species
Must turn to is that earth
Where the dump and the refuge are relations under the sun.

NOTES

Michilimackinac, in "The Continent as the Letter M," is pronounced *mish-illiMACKinaw*.

"Great Fennville Swamp" is the title of a drawing by Philip Bornarth.

"Blue Poles" is the title of a painting by Jackson Pollock.

ACKNOWLEDGMENTS

The poems in this collection first appeared from 1974 to 2000 in the following publications. Grateful acknowledgment remembers the editors of *The American Poetry Review*: "Cuylerville" (section 2 of "Six Places in New York State"), "Heron Weather," "In Defense of Ellis Hollow Creek," "There Is No Real Peace in the World"; *American Review*: "Blue Poles"; *The KGB Bar Book of Poems*: "Astropastoral"; *Lit*: "The pays d'en haut Sublime"; *The Nation*: "Sagg Beach"; *The New Yorker*: "Color Peak Weekend," "Toronto Means the Meeting Place"; *Oxford Poetry* (U.K.): "True Solar Holiday"; *Parenthèse*: "Life in a Small Neighborhood," "The One Who Crossed the Hudson," "To a Watertower"; *The Paris Review*: "Abraham Lincoln in Cleveland," "The Continent as the Letter M," "Theme Park"; *Partisan Review*: "America Began in Houses"; *Poetry*: "Pultneyville," "The Pinnacle Range," "Genesee Falls," "Chimney Bluff" (sections 3 through 6 of "Six Places in New York State"), "Chelsea Square," "The Day Line," "Experience and What To Make of It," "Gunpowder Morning in a Gray Room," "The House at Sagg," "In the Fall When It's Time To Leave," "The Lake Effect," "Locale," "The Revisionist," "The Winter House"; *Poetry in Motion*: "Once the Sole Province"; *Poetry Northwest*: "Covenant," "In Memory of My Country," "Replevin," "Trover"; *Shenandoah*: "Felix Culpa Returns from France"; *Some Other Magazine*: "Creation du Monde"; *William and Mary Review*: "Refuge"; *Yale Review*: "To the Light Fantastic"; *ZZZ*: "Saggaponnack" (section 1 of "Six Places in New York State"), "Great Fennville Swamp," "Summer"; and *ZZZZZ*: "The Elegy for New York," "When Spring Comes First to West 21st Street," "Whiteout."

Several poems have meanwhile been reprinted in other publications, including *The Agriculture Reader*: "The Revisionist"; *American Poetry Annual*

1986: "Theme Park;" *The Best American Poetry 1988*: "True Solar Holiday"; *The Best American Poetry 1989*: "Dog Star Sale"; *The Best of the Best American Poetry*: "True Solar Holiday"; *The Body Electric*: "There Is No Real Peace in the World"; *The Contemporary Landscape* (Hirschl and Adler Gallery): "The Continent as the Letter M"; *Conversation Pieces: Poems That Talk To Other Poems*: "Covenant"; *Ecstatic Occasions, Expedient Forms*: "Once the Sole Province"; *The Forgotten Language*: "In Memory of My Country," "The Revisionist" section 1; *For James Merrill*: "Connecticut"; *Fruta Temporada* (in Spanish): "Heron Weather"; *Harper's*: "America Began in Houses"; *Litoral* (in Spanish): "Color Peak Weekend," "The Continent as the Letter M," "True Solar Holiday"; *The Making of a Poem: A Norton Anthology of Poetic Forms*: "The Elegy for New York"; *The Norton Anthology of American Literature, vol. 2* (second ed.): "The Revisionist" sections 1 and 5 through 8; *The Norton Anthology of Poetry* (third ed.): "Heron Weather," "Summer"; *The Oxford Book of American Poetry*: "Astropastoral," "The Continent as the Letter M," "There Is No Real Peace in the World"; *Some Poets and Painters of the Hampton Landscape* (Elaine Benson Gallery): "Sagg Beach"; *Spazio Umano* (in Italian): "Once the Sole Province," "True Solar Holiday"; *Yale Review*: "True Solar Holiday"; and *The Wadsworth Anthology of Poetry*: "Covenant."

"Connecticut" first appeared as a broadside published on the occasion of a joint reading with Jordan Smith at the Folger Shakespeare Library in Washington, D.C., introduced by Anthony Hecht. "Theme Park" was reprinted as a broadside designed and set by James Walsh on the occasion of a joint reading with Susan Howe at the Center for Book Arts in New York, introduced by Jen Bervin.

"Chelsea Square" inspired the solo piano piece of the same name composed by Jeff Nichols, premiered by Marilyn Nonken at the Miller Theater of Columbia University and included in her album *American Spiritual: New Piano Works*. "True Solar Holiday" inspired the electro-acoustical composition "True Holiday," written and performed by the Berlin-based group The Magic I.D. with lyrics written and sung by Margareth Kammerer, included in their album *till my breath gives out*.

Grateful acknowledgment is extended also to the late editors Roger Donald, who accepted *The Revisionist* for publication by Little, Brown and Company in 1981, and William Corbett, who took *The Astropastorals* for Pressed Wafer in 2017.

DOUGLAS CRASE was born in 1944 in Battle Creek, Michigan, raised on a farm, and educated at Princeton. He has been described in the *Times Literary Supplement* as "the unusual case of a contemporary poet whose most public, expansive voice is his most authentic." His first collection, *The Revisionist*, was nominated for the National Book Critics Circle Award and National (then called American) Book Award, named a Notable Book of the Year in 1981 by *The New York Times*, and earned a Witter Bynner Prize from the American Academy and Institute of Arts and Letters. His chapbook *The Astropastorals* was named a 2017 Book of the Year in the *Times Literary Supplement*. And his collected poems, *The Revisionist and The Astropastorals*, was nominated for a Lambda Literary Award and named a 2019 Book of the Year in both the *Times Literary Supplement* and *Hyperallergic*. He has received an Ingram Merrill Award, Whiting Writers' Award, a Guggenheim Fellowship, and was a MacArthur Fellow from 1987 to 1992. He lives with his husband, Frank Polach, in New York and Carley Brook, Pennsylvania.

MARK FORD was born in 1962 in Nairobi, Kenya, and educated at Oxford. He is considered one of the U.K.'s most distinctive poets and his recent collection, *Enter, Fleeing,* appeared in 2018. A *Selected Poems* was published to acclaim in the U.S. in 2014. He has written two critical biographies, *Raymond Roussel and the Republic of Dreams* and *Thomas Hardy: Half a Londoner*. He lives in London and teaches at University College London.

NIGHTBOAT BOOKS

Nightboat Books, a nonprofit organization, seeks to develop audiences for writers whose work resists convention and transcends boundaries. We publish books rich with poignancy, intelligence, and risk. Please visit nightboat.org to learn about our titles and how you can support our future publications.

The following individuals have supported the publication of this book. We thank them for their generosity and commitment to the mission of Nightboat Books:

Kazim Ali
Anonymous
Jean C. Ballantyne
Photios Giovanis
Amanda Greenberger
Anne Marie Macari
Elizabeth Motika
Benjamin Taylor
Jerrie Whitfield & Richard Motika

In addition, this book has been made possible, in part, by grants from the New York City Department of Cultural Affairs in partnership with the City Council and the New York State Council on the Arts Literature Program.